# GROWING
# HERBS

Deni Bown

**DORLING KINDERSLEY**
London • New York • Stuttgart

A DORLING KINDERSLEY BOOK

**Project Editor**
Martha Swift
**Art Editor**
Alison Verity
**Managing Editor**
Krystyna Mayer
**Managing Art Editor**
Derek Coombes
**DTP Designer**
Cressida Joyce
**Production Controller**
Ruth Charlton

First published in
Great Britain in 1995
by Dorling Kindersley Limited,
9 Henrietta Street,
London WC2E 8PS

Copyright © 1995
Dorling Kindersley Limited,
London
Text copyright © 1995 Deni Bown

A CIP catalogue record for this
book is available from
the British Library

ISBN 0 7513 0216 3

Colour reproduced by
Euroscan, Nottingham,
Great Britain

Printed and bound in Singapore
by Tien Wah Press

# CONTENTS

# INTRODUCTION

*Herb growing has a special appeal, being both practical and enjoyable. Although herbs are valued primarily for their culinary, healing, and cosmetic uses, they also have the charm of wild flowers and evocative scents, so giving the herb garden its uniquely restful atmosphere.*

SOME OF THE EARLIEST HERB GARDENS were planted 2,000 years ago in Egypt. They consisted of geometric beds, and were enclosed by walls to give protection against animals, and make the best use of shelter and water. Herbs were especially important in ritual; for example, chamomile was an ingredient of the embalming oil used to mummify pharaohs. Christian monasteries began in northern Egypt in AD 305. Monastic rule dictated that they grew culinary and medicinal herbs and aromatics for incense, as well as vegetables, fruit, and dye plants. The 9th-century plan for St. Gall, Switzerland,

shows an enclosed garden and rectangular beds, designed along Egyptian lines. It was copied throughout Europe. The list of "herbs both beautiful and health-giving" included savory, rose, sage, fennel, tansy, peppermint, rosemary, parsley, dill, and poppies. All are described in this book. Herb growing today is more flexible in design and purpose, from entire herb gardens to containers. Whatever the scale, it is satisfying to create a pleasing effect. To help you choose suitable plants, this book describes 60 different herbs and more than 100 variations, all of which are easy to grow, even by beginners.

**A WALLED TOWN GARDEN**
*Herb gardens in medieval times followed monastic designs, with small, rectangular beds enclosed by walls or fences.*

# Types of Herb Garden

*The only definition of a herb garden is that it is where herbs are grown. It might be based on a formal design, such as a knot garden or a simple border. At its smallest, it can consist of a window-box, a cartwheel, or a collection of herbs in pots.*

THE TRADITIONAL HERB GARDEN IS usually divided by paths into orderly, geometric beds. It is usually enclosed, with a central feature and somewhere sheltered to sit, making a peaceful retreat. The beds may be raised, to give better drainage, and edged by tiles or timber to hold the soil. Tudor gardens were often framed by low

**AN OPEN KNOT GARDEN**
The pattern in this walled garden is defined by paths made from old bricks, which soften the geometric lines and create a walkway through the herbs.

hedges of aromatic herbs, such as lavender, on which washing was spread out to dry. Designs based on dwarf hedges are known as knot gardens; the beds are either planted with herbs or filled with gravel. Few original knot gardens remain, but recreations have been made in some large gardens, and at many herb nurseries. Larger, more elaborate knot gardens are known as parterres.

### INFORMAL DESIGNS
An informal herb garden, planted in the relaxed style of a herbaceous border or cottage garden, gives scope for creating effects based on complementary habits and colours. It can include herbs that might be out of place in a formal garden, such as large shrubs, invasive mints, giant angelica, or small,

creeping thymes. A compromise between formal and informal is often successful. The Queen's Garden at Kew in west London has a formal structure of terraces above a sunken garden, which consists of two large, rectangular beds. Plantings are all informal, displaying herbs of the 17th century.

### HERBS WITH OTHER GARDEN PLANTS
In many gardens, herbs have to take their places beside other kinds of plant. Many herbs are ornamental border plants in their own right – bergamot, rue, and purple sage are obvious examples. Various thymes are often sold as rock-garden plants, and creeping herbs of all kinds can be planted in gravel or paving to form a fragrant carpet that stands the occasional

**STRAWBERRY POT**
This is an attractive and practical way of growing seven or more herbs vertically. A pot made from terracotta is much more stable than a plastic one.

## HOW THIS BOOK WORKS

This book contains 60 of the most common and easily grown herbs, which are arranged alphabetically by their scientific names. The sample page below shows a typical entry.

**SAMPLE PAGE**

*Herb number corresponds to number on pull-out chart (see below)*

*Scientific name*

*Common name*

*Scientific family name*

*Description of plant's history and uses*

*Planting tips and associations*

*Related species, forms, varieties, hybrids, or cultivars*

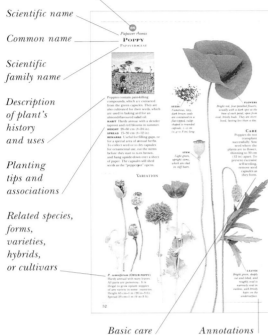

*Basic care information*

*Annotations describing each part of plant in detail*

**PULL-OUT CHART**

The chart lists herbs from 1 to 60. The numbers correspond with the numbers for the herb entries in the book *(see sample page above)*.

*When chart is pulled down, purple strip indicates herb for which cultivation details are displayed below*

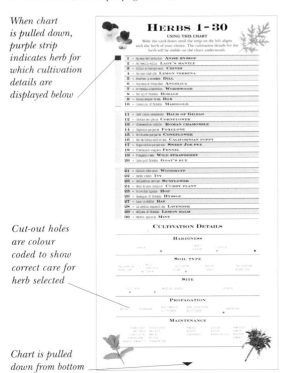

*Cut-out holes are colour coded to show correct care for herb selected*

*Chart is pulled down from bottom*

## DEFINING A HERB

There are two distinct meanings of the word "herb". One is botanical, meaning a non-woody plant, from which we get the term "herbaceous"; and the other refers to any plant that has therapeutic properties. Although we tend to think of herbs as small, aromatic plants, such as parsley and thyme, they include a very wide range of plants, from annuals, biennials, and herbaceous perennials to trees, shrubs, climbers, and primitive plants, such as ferns and mosses. Some herbs are not especially aromatic, and others may even smell unpleasant – for example, a box hedge after clipping.

### SCIENTIFIC TERMS

Just as we devise a family tree to explain our origins, plants are classified according to their relationships, which are based mainly on the structure of floral parts. The classification gives each plant a scientific name in Latin, which is accepted worldwide. This eliminates misunderstandings that would occur if common names in different languages were used.
A plant's scientific name has two main parts, rather like a surname and a first name, for example, *Symphytum officinale*.

The basic relationships are:

**FAMILY**
A group of related genera. Example: Boraginaceae.

**GENUS (plural GENERA)**
A group of related species, indicated by the first part of the Latin name. Example: *Symphytum*.

**SPECIES**
Individuals that are alike and naturally breed with each other, denoted by the second part of the Latin name. Examples: *Symphytum asperum* (Prickly comfrey) or *Symphytum officinale* (Common comfrey).

**HYBRID**
A cross between two species, which sometimes happens in the wild, but more usually occurs accidentally or artificially in cultivation. It is given a different name from either parent, with an "x" to show hybrid status. Example: *Symphytum* X *uplandicum* (Russian comfrey). Parents are sometimes given in brackets after the hybrid name. Example: *Symphytum* X *uplandicum* (*S. asperum* X *S. officinale*).

**VARIETY, SUBSPECIES, AND FORM**
(often given as var., subsp., ssp., forma, or f.) Subdivisions within a species or natural hybrid that differ consistently in small but distinct ways from the type. These natural variants are often rare in the wild, but common in cultivation, offering attractive differences in habit, colour, and so on. Example: *Symphytum officinale* var. *ochroleucum* (White-flowered comfrey).

**CULTIVAR**
A variant produced and maintained by cultivation, which has desirable characteristics of habit, colour, and flavour.
Example: *Symphytum* X *uplandicum* 'Variegatum' (Variegated Russian comfrey).

# CREATING A HERB GARDEN

*Whatever the style of herb garden, much satisfaction
comes from planting the herbs in attractive combinations.
There is a wide choice of herbs to grow, especially
of variants that have different habits and colours,
and often make better garden plants than the wild species.*

Most herbs prefer an open, sunny, well-drained site, and neutral to alkaline soil. Plan the layout of the garden carefully, drawing it to scale if necessary. Remember that small beds give easier access for maintenance and harvesting than large ones, and provide stepping stones in large beds to prevent trampling and compaction. Transfer the design to the ground, using pegs and string, before making beds and paths. Prepare the soil by removing weeds,

**GOLDEN BORDER**
This border combines fennel (*Foeniculum vulgare*) and tansy (*Tanacetum vulgare*) with golden hop (*Humulus lupulus* 'Aureus') and golden marjoram (*Origanum vulgare* 'Aureum'). The colours are complementary, and there are strong contrasts in shape and texture.

and then by forking in manure or compost. Drainage can be improved by adding grit, and by raising or sloping the beds.

### CHOOSING HERBS

Herb nurseries offer the widest range of herbs, but garden centres are good for popular herbs and for variants that may suit certain situations. Upright, prostrate, and compact variants give contrasts in height and shape; variants with bronze, variegated, or golden foliage inspire exciting colour schemes. Before buying, check the requirements of each herb.

**CREEPING THYMES**
*These soften the wooden edging and are good for gaps in the paving.*

**HOUSELEEK**
*Like creeping thymes, houseleeks enjoy dry, sunny conditions at the edges of paths.*

**HERBS IN THE BORDER**
This scheme makes use of contrasting heights, habits, and colours. Each herb is allowed sufficient space for its height and spread, giving good ground cover without overcrowding. The raised bed has a wooden edging to retain the soil, and is accessed by paths.

footstep. Small, neat herbs are suitable for edging; wall germander is good beside paths, and culinary herbs, such as curly parsley and chives, are attractive around a vegetable plot. Scented pelargoniums and colourful annuals, such as poppies and cornflowers, are useful for filling gaps

**HANGING BASKET**
This is a good way of growing small and compact herbs, although they must be resilient to withstand wind damage.

Growing herbs in containers has several advantages – the plants are easy to replace so at least one can always be at its best, and all but the largest containers are moveable. The only disadvantages are that the plants require regular watering and feeding, and need repotting or replacing every spring. Containers are especially useful for certain herbs. They are ideal for confining invasive mints, and for leafy culinary herbs, such as basil. Containerized specimen shrubs of box or bay, clipped into topiary shapes, create instant focal points. If grown in pots, frost-hardy herbs, such as lemon verbena and myrtle, can be conveniently brought under cover in cold weather. A window-box, hanging basket, or strawberry pot

**HERB TOWER**
Chives, thyme, marjoram, mint, purple sage, and parsley have been planted in this container, which was constructed from moss and chicken-wire.

in a border. Lavender and rosemary are most enjoyed near a seat or entrance, where a sprig can be picked as you pass.

## HERBS IN CONTAINERS
Many herbs grow well in containers. In small gardens or on balconies, the entire herb garden may consist of containers, imaginatively positioned on walls, steps, shelves, and window-sills. Almost any container is suitable, provided that it has drainage holes to prevent waterlogging.

**FORMAL ARRANGEMENT**
A neat way of growing a variety of herbs in a formal manner is to plant them in a small, circular, brick-edged bed.

(a large pot with planting pockets), planted with a collection of herbs, makes an interesting feature that takes up little space. When planting a mixture of herbs in the same container, try to include small-growing types and to avoid very tall herbs.

## PLANTING

Like any plant, herbs will do best in the right conditions. For example, Mediterranean herbs enjoy dry, sunny positions, woodland herbs prefer dappled shade, and variegated and golden variants retain their colours best in positions shaded at midday. Take note of the eventual height and spread, since a common mistake is to plant too close together. Container-grown herbs can be planted at any time, but will establish quickest in spring. If kept under cover, they should be acclimatized ("hardened off") before planting. First set out the plants in their pots to check arrangement and planting distances. Water them thoroughly before planting, as dry root balls are difficult to wet once below ground, and again after planting to provide even moisture for root growth. Pinch out any growing tips to encourage new sideshoots and a bushy habit.

### MIXED COLOURS

The small, colourful flowers of heartsease (*Viola tricolor*) are given greater impact by a background of purple sage (*Salvia officinalis* 'Purpurascens').

## MAINTENANCE

Most herbs are naturally vigorous and will require little attention when established. Maintenance consists largely of cutting back plants in winter to remove dead stems, and in spring and summer to encourage strong new growth. Dead-heading prolongs flowering and prevents excessive self-seeding. Clump-forming perennials need dividing every few years to maintain vigour. Invasive herbs, such as mints and tansy, may need annual division and removal of excessive new growth. Mulch the herb garden in spring with a layer of well-rotted manure or compost. If pests or diseases become a problem, improve ventilation and feeding, but use only organic sprays on herbs that will be harvested. In cold areas, or severe frost, protect vulnerable herbs with a layer of straw or dead leaves around the base and some horticultural fleece over the foliage.

### VARIEGATED RUE

*This variegated plant, with some completely white leaves, stands out well against simpler, darker foliage. It should be pruned hard in spring to retain its variegation.*

### GOLD-VARIEGATED SAGE

*An excellent plant for the fronts of borders, since it retains its habit and colour well. It will also add colour to pots of plain green culinary herbs.*

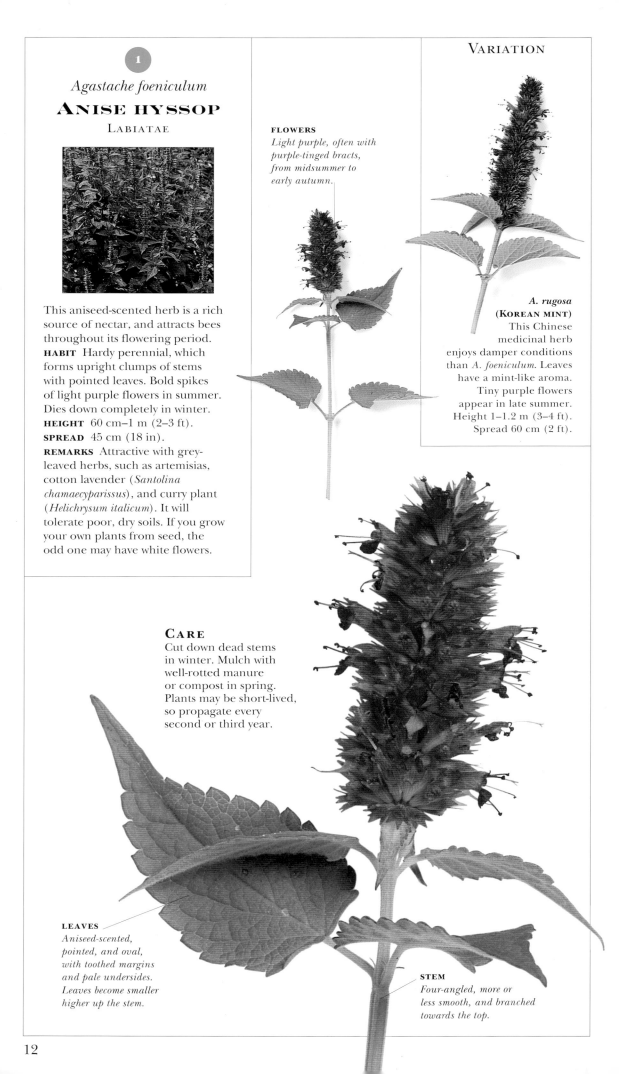

**1**

*Agastache foeniculum*

# ANISE HYSSOP

LABIATAE

This aniseed-scented herb is a rich source of nectar, and attracts bees throughout its flowering period.
**HABIT** Hardy perennial, which forms upright clumps of stems with pointed leaves. Bold spikes of light purple flowers in summer. Dies down completely in winter.
**HEIGHT** 60 cm–1 m (2–3 ft).
**SPREAD** 45 cm (18 in).
**REMARKS** Attractive with grey-leaved herbs, such as artemisias, cotton lavender (*Santolina chamaecyparissus*), and curry plant (*Helichrysum italicum*). It will tolerate poor, dry soils. If you grow your own plants from seed, the odd one may have white flowers.

**FLOWERS**
*Light purple, often with purple-tinged bracts, from midsummer to early autumn.*

### VARIATION

*A. rugosa*
(**KOREAN MINT**)
This Chinese medicinal herb enjoys damper conditions than *A. foeniculum*. Leaves have a mint-like aroma. Tiny purple flowers appear in late summer. Height 1–1.2 m (3–4 ft). Spread 60 cm (2 ft).

### CARE
Cut down dead stems in winter. Mulch with well-rotted manure or compost in spring. Plants may be short-lived, so propagate every second or third year.

**LEAVES**
*Aniseed-scented, pointed, and oval, with toothed margins and pale undersides. Leaves become smaller higher up the stem.*

**STEM**
*Four-angled, more or less smooth, and branched towards the top.*

**FLOWERS**
*Tiny, pale lilac to white, appearing in loose spikes during summer.*

**4**

*Aloysia triphylla*

# LEMON VERBENA

### VERBENACEAE

**LEAVES**
*Slender and light green, up to 10 cm (4 in) long, and short-stalked. Leaves are arranged in threes, and have a rough texture and a strong lemon scent.*

This South American shrub has a delicious lemon scent. The dried leaves retain their fragrance well, and are useful ingredients of pot-pourris and tisanes.

**HABIT** Frost-hardy, deciduous shrub, with tiny flowers in summer.

**HEIGHT** 1–3 m (3–10 ft).

**SPREAD** 1–3 m (3–10 ft).

**REMARKS** Needs a warm, sheltered position in cold areas. Frosted plants may be slow to recover, but usually sprout from the base by early summer. Grow pots of lemon verbena near seats and entrances, or plant in containers with black basil (*Ocimum basilicum* 'Dark Opal').

## CARE

Cut back main stems to 30 cm (12 in), and side shoots to within two or three buds of the old wood in spring. Remove dead wood in early summer. Repot container-grown plants in spring, or topdress with fresh compost. Remove dead flower heads and trim untidy shoots after flowering.

**STEM**
*Slender, brown, and woody.*

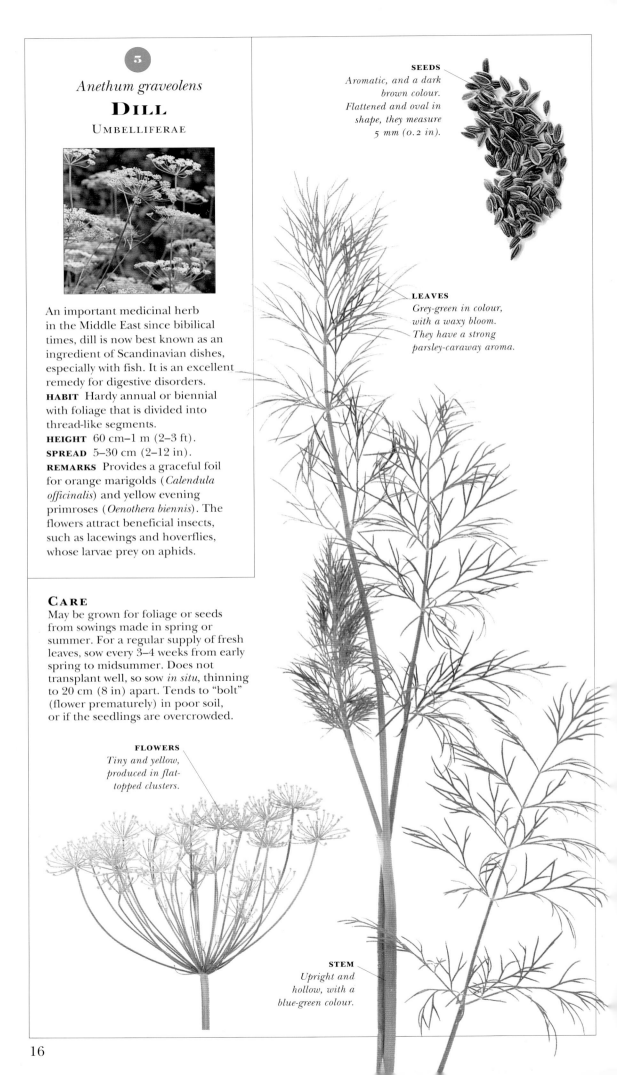

**5**

*Anethum graveolens*

# DILL

UMBELLIFERAE

**SEEDS**
*Aromatic, and a dark brown colour. Flattened and oval in shape, they measure 5 mm (0.2 in).*

An important medicinal herb in the Middle East since bibilical times, dill is now best known as an ingredient of Scandinavian dishes, especially with fish. It is an excellent remedy for digestive disorders.
**HABIT** Hardy annual or biennial with foliage that is divided into thread-like segments.
**HEIGHT** 60 cm–1 m (2–3 ft).
**SPREAD** 5–30 cm (2–12 in).
**REMARKS** Provides a graceful foil for orange marigolds (*Calendula officinalis*) and yellow evening primroses (*Oenothera biennis*). The flowers attract beneficial insects, such as lacewings and hoverflies, whose larvae prey on aphids.

**LEAVES**
*Grey-green in colour, with a waxy bloom. They have a strong parsley-caraway aroma.*

## CARE
May be grown for foliage or seeds from sowings made in spring or summer. For a regular supply of fresh leaves, sow every 3–4 weeks from early spring to midsummer. Does not transplant well, so sow *in situ*, thinning to 20 cm (8 in) apart. Tends to "bolt" (flower prematurely) in poor soil, or if the seedlings are overcrowded.

**FLOWERS**
*Tiny and yellow, produced in flat-topped clusters.*

**STEM**
*Upright and hollow, with a blue-green colour.*

**LEAVES**
*Aromatic and long-stalked. They are deeply divided and have irregular toothed margins.*

## 6

*Angelica archangelica*
# ANGELICA
UMBELLIFERAE

Angelica was known as *herba angelica* (angelic herb) in medieval times, because it was believed to cure all ills. An important medicinal herb, it can be used to flavour liqueurs, or candied for cake decoration.
**HABIT** Giant, hardy biennial, or short-lived perennial. Tiny, green-white flowers appear in flat-topped clusters in late spring and summer.
**HEIGHT** 1–2.5 m (3–8 ft).
**SPREAD** 45 cm–1.2 m (18 in–4 ft).
**REMARKS** An architectural plant for the back of the border. It overpowers most smaller herbs, but is a match for Sweet Joe Pye (*Eupatorium purpureum*). It may self-sow prolifically.

**SEEDS**
*Oval-oblong and flattened, with winged ridges. Sow angelica seeds when fresh, since they do not store well.*

## CARE
Make sure that seedlings have sufficient room to develop, since they can smother smaller plants. Remove dead flower heads to prevent excessive self-seeding, or cut and dry seed heads for ornament while the seeds are still green and unripe. Mulch second-year plants with well-rotted manure or compost in spring to produce very large plants.

**STEM**
*Green, hollow, and ridged, this can be up to 6 cm (2.4 in) in diameter.*

*Artemisia absinthium*
# WORMWOOD
COMPOSITAE

Artemisias include some of the bitterest herbs known; hence the expression "as bitter as wormwood", dating to biblical times. Wormwood was used as a household remedy to stimulate the digestive system.
**HABIT** Hardy, shrubby perennial, with grey-green foliage and tiny, dull yellow flowers in summer.
**HEIGHT** 1 m (3 ft).
**SPREAD** 25 cm–1 m (10–36 in).
**REMARKS** An excellent, easily grown plant for poor, dry soils. Effective in a white border, and also with dark-leaved plants, such as bronze fennel (*Foeniculum vulgare* 'Purpureum'). May also be planted as an informal hedge.

**A. caucasica**
(SYN. **A. lanata**)
Tufted, mat-forming, hardy shrublet with finely cut, fern-like foliage, silver-green in colour, and aromatic. Loose clusters of tiny, round yellow flowers in summer. Good for edging. Height and spread 15–30 cm (6–12 in).

**A. arborescens**
Half-hardy, aromatic, shrubby perennial with a rounded habit. It is recommended for alkaline soils. Height and spread 1.1 m (3.5 ft).

**LEAVES**
*Aromatic, silver-green, silky, and finely divided into narrow segments.*

**FLOWERS**
*Tiny, nodding yellow flowers in slender clusters, which give a graceful effect.*

**STEM**
*Upright and grooved to angled, light green with a silky hairy texture, becoming woody at the base.*

**A. a. 'LAMBROOK SILVER'**
This has luxuriant, silver-grey foliage. It makes a good background for red-purple herbs. Height 45–80 cm (18–32 in). Spread 50 cm (20 in).

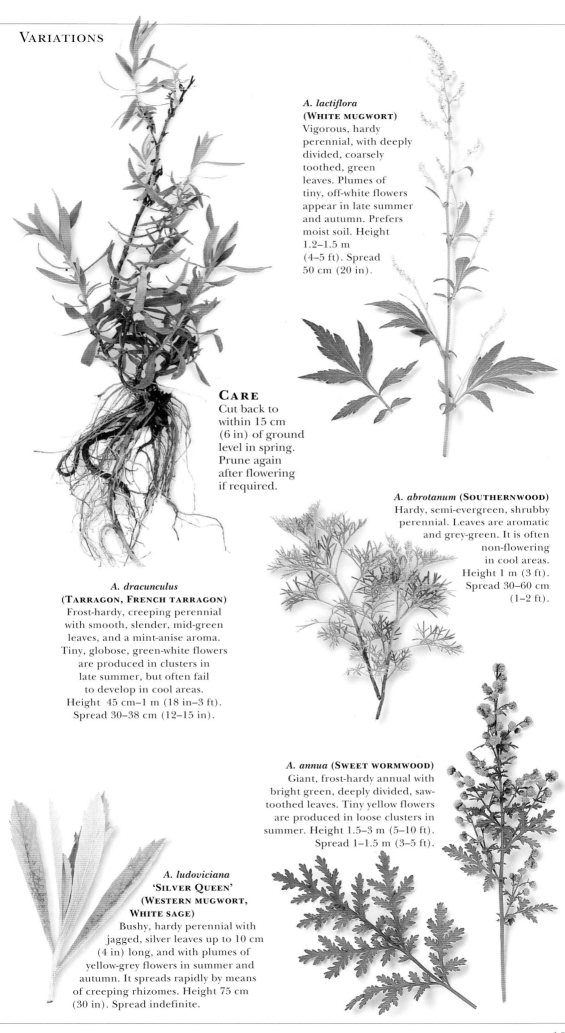

## VARIATIONS

**A. lactiflora**
(**WHITE MUGWORT**)
Vigorous, hardy
perennial, with deeply
divided, coarsely
toothed, green
leaves. Plumes of
tiny, off-white flowers
appear in late summer
and autumn. Prefers
moist soil. Height
1.2–1.5 m
(4–5 ft). Spread
50 cm (20 in).

### CARE
Cut back to
within 15 cm
(6 in) of ground
level in spring.
Prune again
after flowering
if required.

**A. abrotanum** (**SOUTHERNWOOD**)
Hardy, semi-evergreen, shrubby
perennial. Leaves are aromatic
and grey-green. It is often
non-flowering
in cool areas.
Height 1 m (3 ft).
Spread 30–60 cm
(1–2 ft).

**A. dracunculus**
(**TARRAGON, FRENCH TARRAGON**)
Frost-hardy, creeping perennial
with smooth, slender, mid-green
leaves, and a mint-anise aroma.
Tiny, globose, green-white flowers
are produced in clusters in
late summer, but often fail
to develop in cool areas.
Height 45 cm–1 m (18 in–3 ft).
Spread 30–38 cm (12–15 in).

**A. annua** (**SWEET WORMWOOD**)
Giant, frost-hardy annual with
bright green, deeply divided, saw-
toothed leaves. Tiny yellow flowers
are produced in loose clusters in
summer. Height 1.5–3 m (5–10 ft).
Spread 1–1.5 m (3–5 ft).

**A. ludoviciana**
'**SILVER QUEEN**'
(**WESTERN MUGWORT,**
**WHITE SAGE**)
Bushy, hardy perennial with
jagged, silver leaves up to 10 cm
(4 in) long, and with plumes of
yellow-grey flowers in summer and
autumn. It spreads rapidly by means
of creeping rhizomes. Height 75 cm
(30 in). Spread indefinite.

## *Borago officinalis*
# BORAGE
### BORAGINACEAE

Fresh borage flowers and leaves
have been added to wine and
salads since classical times. The
seeds contain an oil, rich in
linolenic acid, which has similar
effects to evening primrose oil.
**HABIT** Hardy annual with coarsely
hairy, cucumber-scented leaves,
and bright blue, star-shaped
flowers throughout the summer.
**HEIGHT** 30 cm–1 m (1–3 ft).
**SPREAD** 15–30 cm (6–12 in).
**REMARKS** The bright blue flowers
of borage make a brilliant contrast
to orange marigolds (*Calendula
officinalis*), Californian poppies
(*Eschscholzia californica*), and
corn poppies (*Papaver rhoeas*).

## CARE
Sow borage *in situ*,
since it forms a
stout taproot and
will not transplant
well. Thin seedlings
to 45 cm (18 in)
apart. Self-sows in
most gardens.
Plants tend to
flop, and usually
need staking. The
bristly foliage can
cause skin irritation.

**FLOWERS**
*Bright blue, five-petalled,
and star-shaped, fading
to white in the centre,
and with conspicuous
black stamen tips.*

**LEAVES**
*Mid-green, oval, and
pointed, with a rough,
bristly texture.
They smell and
taste of cucumber.*

**STEM**
*Stout, hollow,
and clad in
bristly white
hairs. It is
upright at first,
branching and
leaning as it
develops.*

**SEEDS**
*Relatively large nutlets,
5–8 mm (0.2–0.3 in) in
length, and almost black.
Viable for eight years if
kept in a cool, dry place.*

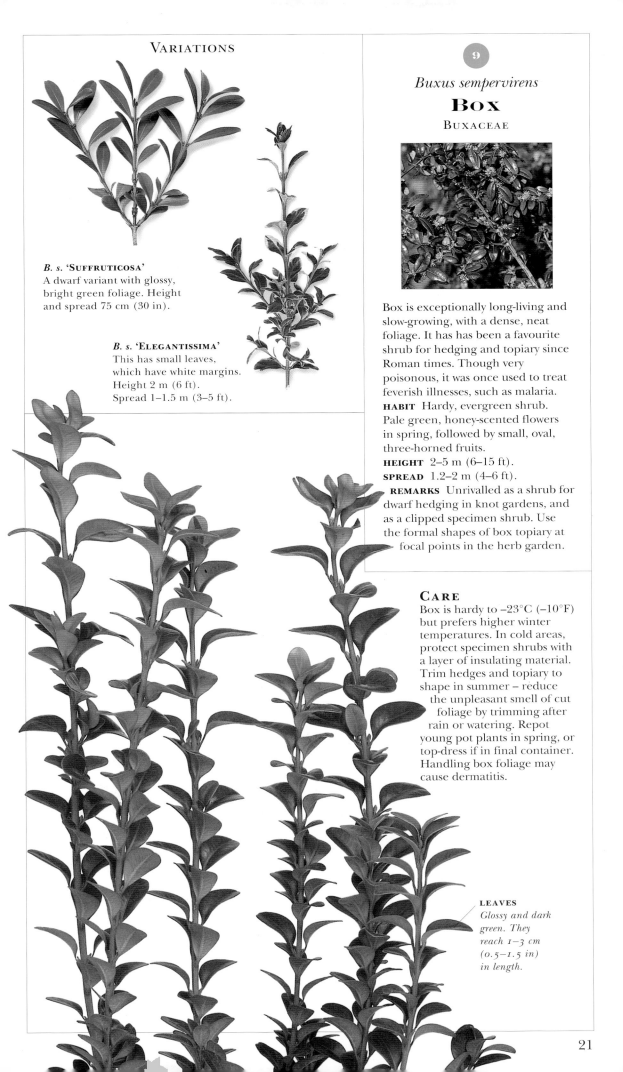

## VARIATIONS

**B. s. 'SUFFRUTICOSA'**
A dwarf variant with glossy, bright green foliage. Height and spread 75 cm (30 in).

**B. s. 'ELEGANTISSIMA'**
This has small leaves, which have white margins. Height 2 m (6 ft). Spread 1–1.5 m (3–5 ft).

*Buxus sempervirens*

# BOX

BUXACEAE

Box is exceptionally long-living and slow-growing, with a dense, neat foliage. It has has been a favourite shrub for hedging and topiary since Roman times. Though very poisonous, it was once used to treat feverish illnesses, such as malaria.

**HABIT** Hardy, evergreen shrub. Pale green, honey-scented flowers in spring, followed by small, oval, three-horned fruits.

**HEIGHT** 2–5 m (6–15 ft).

**SPREAD** 1.2–2 m (4–6 ft).

**REMARKS** Unrivalled as a shrub for dwarf hedging in knot gardens, and as a clipped specimen shrub. Use the formal shapes of box topiary at focal points in the herb garden.

## CARE

Box is hardy to –23°C (–10°F) but prefers higher winter temperatures. In cold areas, protect specimen shrubs with a layer of insulating material. Trim hedges and topiary to shape in summer – reduce the unpleasant smell of cut foliage by trimming after rain or watering. Repot young pot plants in spring, or top-dress if in final container. Handling box foliage may cause dermatitis.

**LEAVES**
*Glossy and dark green. They reach 1–3 cm (0.5–1.5 in) in length.*

*Calendula officinalis*
# MARIGOLD
### COMPOSITAE

This colourful, versatile herb is very easy to grow, and blooms continuously, providing an almost year-round supply of petals for colouring and flavouring in the kitchen, or for simple skin preparations.

**HABIT** Hardy, long-lived, aromatic annual with a bushy habit.

**HEIGHT** 50–70 cm (20–28 in).

**SPREAD** 50–70 cm (20–28 in).

**REMARKS** Plant marigolds with borage (*Borago officinalis*) and cornflowers (*Centaurea cyanea*), or create dramatic contrast with a background of fennel (*Foeniculum vulgare* 'Purpureum') or elder (*Sambucus nigra* 'Guincho Purple').

**SEED HEAD**
*This contains the seeds, which can easily be collected for growing the following year.*

**LEAVES**
*Light green in colour, with a narrow-oblong shape. They reach 5–17 cm (2–7 in) in length.*

**SEEDS**
*Light brown and C-shaped. They can be up to 5 mm (0.2 in) in length.*

**FLOWERS**
*Yellow-orange ray florets (a source of yellow dye) with central yellow-orange to brown disks.*

**STEM**
*Branched and more or less upright.*

## CARE
Sow in autumn for very early flowers, and again in spring for blooming throughout summer and autumn. Removing dead flower heads prolongs flowering and prevents excessive self-seeding.

**FLOWERS**
*Terminal clusters of pink to lilac, tubular, two-lipped flowers, about 1 cm (0.4 in) long, and opening in succession.*

**LEAVES**
*Trifoliate, and up to 10 cm (4 in) in length, with slender-oblong, tapering leaflets, serrated margins, and a cedar-lemon aroma.*

**11**

## *Cedronella canariensis*
# BALM OF GILEAD
### LABIATAE

This is an attractive, aromatic plant for pot-pourris and herb teas, but it is more often grown for its exotic name. True balm of Gilead is a medicinal resin, collected from a desert shrub, *Balsamodendron opobalsamum*, balsam firs (*Abies balsamea*), and various poplars.

**HABIT** Tender, shrubby perennial with strongly scented leaves.

**HEIGHT** 1.5 m (5 ft).

**SPREAD** 1 m (3 ft).

**REMARKS** Grow in frost-free gardens, or in pots for the conservatory or patio, beside scented pelargoniums (*Pelargonium* species), which have similarly interesting aromas.

**STEM**
*Square in cross-section, and ridged with a rough texture.*

## CARE
Cut back hard in spring to encourage new shoots from the base, and lightly again after flowering. Mulch with well-rotted manure or compost in spring. Repot young plants, or top-dress plants in large pots in spring.

## *Centaurea cyanus*
# CORNFLOWER
### COMPOSITAE

Cornflowers are favourite garden annuals, and an easily grown herb that benefits skin, hair, and eyes.

**HABIT** Tall, slender, hardy annual, with bright blue (occasionally white, pink, or purple) flowers on long stalks in summer.

**HEIGHT** 20 cm–1 m (8 in–3 ft).

**SPREAD** 15–30 cm (6–12 in).

**REMARKS** Grow vivid blue cornflowers with scarlet poppies (*Papaver rhoeas*), their natural companions in the wild. For added realism, combine the seeds with a packet of ornamental grasses. They also look good with marigolds (*Calendula officinalis*) and evening primroses (*Oenothera biennis*).

## CARE
Sow in autumn for early flowers the following year, or in spring for summer blooms. For a prolonged flowering period, sow every three weeks from early spring to autumn. They do not transplant well, so sow *in situ* and thin to 23 cm (9 in) apart. They are naturally erect among other plants, but may need staking when exposed. Regular deadheading will extend the flowering period.

**FLOWERS**
*The radiating outer florets are tubular and deeply lobed, surrounding smaller central florets. Flower heads last well in water and retain colour when dried.*

**C. c. 'FLORENCE SERIES'**
A compact variety with blue, pink, carmine, or white flowers.
Height 38–45 cm (15–18 in).
Spread 15–30 cm (6–12 in).

**STEM**
*Long, slender, and grooved, with many wiry branches.*

**LEAVES**
*Linear and slender in shape, these are grey-green in colour, and cottony.*

**FLOWERS**
*Long-stalked, solitary, and daisy-like, with white ray florets that droop as the flower ages. The dome-shaped, central yellow disk is highly aromatic.*

**STEM**
*Thin, wiry, and ridged. It is erect to spreading.*

**SEEDS**
*Light brown in colour, narrow in shape, and minute.*

**LEAVES**
*These are spirally arranged, and finely divided, with an apple scent that fills the air if plants are bruised or trodden upon.*

*Chamaemelum nobile*

# ROMAN CHAMOMILE
### COMPOSITAE

This is an ancient healing herb, still used in remedies for digestive and stress-related disorders, beauty products, and teas. It is known as the "physician plant", since it reputedly improves the health of neighbouring garden plants.

**HABIT** Hardy, mat-forming, evergreen perennial.

**HEIGHT** 15 cm (6 in).

**SPREAD** 45 cm (18 in).

**REMARKS** A prostrate plant that is traditionally planted as a lawn, but is difficult to establish and maintain on a large scale. Instead, plant it in gaps left in patio paving.

## VARIATIONS

*Matricaria recutita* (**GERMAN CHAMOMILE**) This has slender, branched stems, sweetly scented leaves, and aromatic flowers. Height 15–60 cm (6–24 in). Spread 10–38 cm (4–15 in).

*C. n.* '**FLORE PLENO**' (**DOUBLE CHAMOMILE**) This has long-lasting, double cream flowers. It is usually sterile, so should be propagated by division in spring. Height 15 cm (6 in). Spread 45 cm (18 in).

### CARE
Plant 10–15 cm (4–6 in) apart as a "lawn", and weed regularly until well-established. Trim lightly but regularly, using shears, or plant the non-flowering variety 'Treneague', which does not need cutting. Plants may deteriorate in very cold or wet winters, but will usually recover.

*C. n.* '**TRENEAGUE**' (**LAWN CHAMOMILE**)
A non-flowering cultivar that forms a mossy carpet, ideal for lawns, seats, and gaps in paving. Height 2.5 cm (1 in). Spread 45 cm (18 in).

## *Digitalis purpurea*
# FOXGLOVE
SCROPHULARIACEAE

This is a popular, but poisonous, garden plant, grown for its elegant, one-sided spires of tubular flowers. It is the source of important heart drugs, such as digitoxin.

**HABIT** Tall, hardy biennial with tall spikes of flowers in summer.

**HEIGHT** 1–2 m (3–6 ft).

**SPREAD** 30–60 cm (1–2 ft).

**REMARKS** Grow foxgloves among trees and shrubs, at the backs of borders, or where they are illuminated by shafts of early morning or evening sun. Their poisonous foliage is easily confused with that of comfrey (*Symphytum officinale*). Position them out of reach of children and pets.

**LEAVES**
*Oval to slender in shape, they have a soft, thin, and slightly wrinkled texture, with a blunt tip and finely serrated margins.*

### CARE
Foxglove seed is very tiny, and needs light to germinate. For best results, mix with sand, and scatter thinly *in situ*. It will self-sow in most gardens, especially on slightly acid soils.

**FLOWERS**
*Natural variation produces occasional white-flowered plants.*

**FLOWERS**
*Racemes of 20 to 80 purple-pink, tubular flowers, with pale, purple-spotted insides.*

**STEM**
*This is usually solitary, and has a smooth texture.*

**D. lanata**
(**WOOLLY FOXGLOVE**)
Hardy biennial or short-lived perennial, with a purple-tinged stem and narrow leaves.
Height 1 m (3 ft).
Spread 25 cm (10 in).

**D. lutea**
(**STRAW FOXGLOVE**)
Hardy perennial, with smooth, pointed leaves and cream flowers.
Height 75 cm (30 in).
Spread 30 cm (12 in).

**FLOWERS**
*Honey-scented daisies up to 10 cm (4 in) across, with purple-pink ray florets, and conical, dark orange-brown centres.*

*Echinacea purpurea*

# CONEFLOWER

COMPOSITAE

Coneflowers are both beautiful and useful. Once regarded as a cure-all, they are now known to stimulate the immune system and clear toxins from the body. Their magnificent flowers give glowing colour to the herb garden.

**HABIT** Hardy, rhizomatous perennial. Large, scented flowers in summer and early autumn.

**HEIGHT** 1.2 m (4 ft).

**SPREAD** 45 cm (18 in).

**REMARKS** A tall, colourful border plant, effective against herbs such as bronze fennel (*Foeniculum vulgare* 'Purpureum') and purple elder (*Sambucus nigra* 'Guincho Purple').

## CARE

For best results, feed with well-rotted manure or compost in spring. Stake plants securely, early in the season, to prevent flopping as flowering begins. Remove dead flowers regularly to prolong display. Cut back to ground level when foliage has died off in autumn.

**LEAVES**
*These have a slender, oval shape, and are shallow-toothed with a rough texture. They taper to a point, and are up to 15 cm (6 in) long.*

## VARIATION

*E. angustifolia*
(**NARROW-LEAVED CONEFLOWER**)
Very similar to *E. purpurea*, but slightly taller, with slender leaves and drooping, narrower ray florets. Height 1.5 m (5 ft). Spread 45 cm (18 in).

*Eschscholzia californica*

# CALIFORNIAN POPPY

## PAPAVERACEAE

This easily grown annual is the state flower of California. It is a mildly sedative herb, and is used by Native North Americans for toothache.

**HABIT** Hardy, upright to sprawling annual with a long taproot. Vivid flowers of yellow and orange all summer, followed by ribbed capsules up to 10 cm (4 in) long.

**HEIGHT** 20–60 cm (8–24 in).

**SPREAD** 15–30 cm (6–12 in).

**REMARKS** Emphasize the waxy foliage of the Californian poppy by planting with rue (*Ruta graveolens* 'Jackman's Blue') and sorrel (*Rumex scutatus* 'Silver Leaf').

**STEM**
*Slender, brittle, and either upright or spreading.*

**CARE**
Flowers best in dry, sandy, sun-baked conditions. Sow in succession from spring to early summer for a long period of colour. In warm, dry areas, seed may also be sown in late summer for flowers the following spring. Does not transplant successfully, so sow *in situ* and thin to 15 cm (6 in) apart. Self-sows in most gardens.

**FLOWERS**
*Solitary and yellow to orange in colour. Between 5 and 7.5 cm (2–3 in) across, with four petals that curl up in dull weather. For cutting, pick just before opening.*

**LEAVES**
*Smooth, blue-green, and finely cut, with long stalks and a waxy bloom. Easily damaged, and both leaves and stems contain watery latex.*

**SEEDS**
*Dark brown, narrow, and pointed. Up to 3 mm (0.1 in) in length, with a tuft of hairs.*

## CARE
Stake in early summer to prevent wind damage as flowering approaches. Cut down dead stems in winter. Mulch with well-rotted manure or compost in spring.

*Eupatorium purpureum*
# SWEET JOE PYE
COMPOSITAE

This stately, late-flowering, medicinal herb is suited to the backs of large borders. It is named after Jopi, a Native North American who used it to cure typhus.

**HABIT** Hardy perennial with dense clusters of pink flowers in late summer and autumn.

**HEIGHT** 1.2–3 m (4–10 ft).

**SPREAD** 60 cm–1 m (2–3 ft).

**REMARKS** Plant this tall herb with sunflowers (*Helianthus annuus*) and angelica (*Angelica*), or beside shrubby herbs such as elder (*Sambucus nigra*) and Chinese chaste tree (*Vitex negundo*). Try also near purple elder (*Sambucus nigra* 'Guincho Purple').

**FLOWERS**
*Pale pink to purple-pink (occasionally yellow-green or white), appearing in rounded clusters.*

**STEM**
*Stout, upright, and maroon or tinged purple at the nodes.*

**LEAVES**
*Whorls of three to six oval, finely toothed leaves, which have a vanilla scent when crushed.*

## VARIATION

**E. cannabinum (HEMP AGRIMONY)**
Hardy perennial with downy stems. Height 30 cm–1.2 m (1–4 ft). Spread 30–60 cm (1–2 ft).

*Foeniculum vulgare*

# FENNEL

UMBELLIFERAE

Fennel has been grown as a herb and vegetable since classical times. All parts are edible and beneficial, containing an essential oil that improves digestion. It is also indispensable as a garden plant, with delightful feathery foliage.

**HABIT** Hardy perennial with stout stems and glossy leaves.

**HEIGHT** 2 m (6 ft).

**SPREAD** 45 cm (18 in).

**REMARKS** An outstanding border plant because of its stiffly upright stems, which rarely need staking. Plant beside other tall, yellow-flowered herbs, such as evening primroses (*Oenothera biennis*) and mullein (*Verbascum thapsus*).

## CARE

Grow from seed in autumn or spring. Keep well away from dill (*Anethum graveolens*), as they hybridize easily. Though hardy, fennel dislikes cold, damp winters, and may need protecting with a layer of insulating material.

## VARIATION

**F. v. 'PURPUREUM'
(BRONZE FENNEL)**
A favourite cultivar with rich brown foliage. Comes true from seed, and usually self-sows generously. Hardier in cold, damp areas than the species. Height 1.2–1.5 m (4–5 ft). Spread 45 cm (18 in).

**LEAVES**
*Broadly triangular in outline, glossy, and aniseed-scented. Up to 30 cm (12 in) long, and divided into thread-like segments. The leaf stalk clasps the stem.*

**FLOWERS**
*Tiny and dull yellow, appearing in aromatic, flat-topped clusters.*

**STEM**
*Erect, shiny, finely lined, and hollow. It branches at the onset of flowering.*

**SEEDS**
*Oval in shape, pale green-brown, with an aniseed flavour, and a ribbed texture. They measure 4 to 6 mm (0.15–0.2 in).*

## VARIATION

**SEEDS**
*Very small and tear-shaped. They are glossy and pale brown in colour, and are embedded in the skin of the fruit.*

**F. v. 'VARIEGATA'**
This cultivar has cream-edged leaves.
Height 25 cm (10 in).
Spread 20 cm (8 in).

**LEAVES**
*Trifoliate, with oval, deeply veined and toothed leaflets up to 6 cm (2.4 in) long. When thoroughly dried, they can be used in herbal tea mixtures.*

**FLOWERS**
*White, five-petalled, about 0.5 cm (0.2 in) across, and with yellow centres.*

*Fragaria vesca*
# WILD STRAWBERRY
ROSACEAE

Strawberry plants have always been popular household remedies for skin problems and other minor ailments. Fruits of wild strawberries are smaller than those of cultivated varieties, but are very aromatic.
**HABIT** Hardy perennial with long runners, which root where the leaves and stem join. Flowers followed by bright red, oval fruits.
**HEIGHT** 25 cm (10 in).
**SPREAD** 20 cm (8 in).
**REMARKS** A tolerant, easily grown, useful herb, which makes excellent ground cover between taller perennials and beneath shrubs.

**STEM**
*Slender, wiry, and often red-tinged.*

## CARE
May be invasive in some gardens, so remove excess runners as they appear. Fruits are often hidden under the foliage, and are usually safe from birds, but may need protection from slugs. Easily propagated from plantlets at the ends of runners.

## *Galega officinalis*
# GOAT'S RUE
LEGUMINOSAE

This interesting medicinal herb and beautiful border plant has been renowned since ancient times for improving milk yields in cows. The fresh juice is also used to coagulate milk for cheese-making. Its scientific name comes from the Greek word *gala*, meaning milk.

**HABIT** Hardy, bushy perennial, flowering in summer.

**HEIGHT** 1–1.5 m (3–5 ft).

**SPREAD** 60 cm–1 m (2–3 ft).

**REMARKS** Ideal in a mixed border with predominantly red, pink, and purple colouring. Most effective with roses (*Rosa*), coneflowers (*Echinacea purpurea*), and opium poppies (*Papaver somniferum*).

**LEAVES**
*These are smooth, mid-green, and divided into pairs of oblong leaflets, about 5 cm (2 in) long, on either side of the leaf stalk.*

**FLOWERS**
*Lavender to pink-and-white pea flowers in long-stalked racemes, which appear where the leaves meet the stem.*

**STEM**
*More or less upright, branched, hollow, and fairly weak.*

## CARE
Easy and fast-growing from seed or divisions. Sow seed in the open ground in spring, and separate seedlings when large enough to handle. Plant among roses to help support stems, or stake mature plants early in the growing season to prevent flopping as flowering begins.

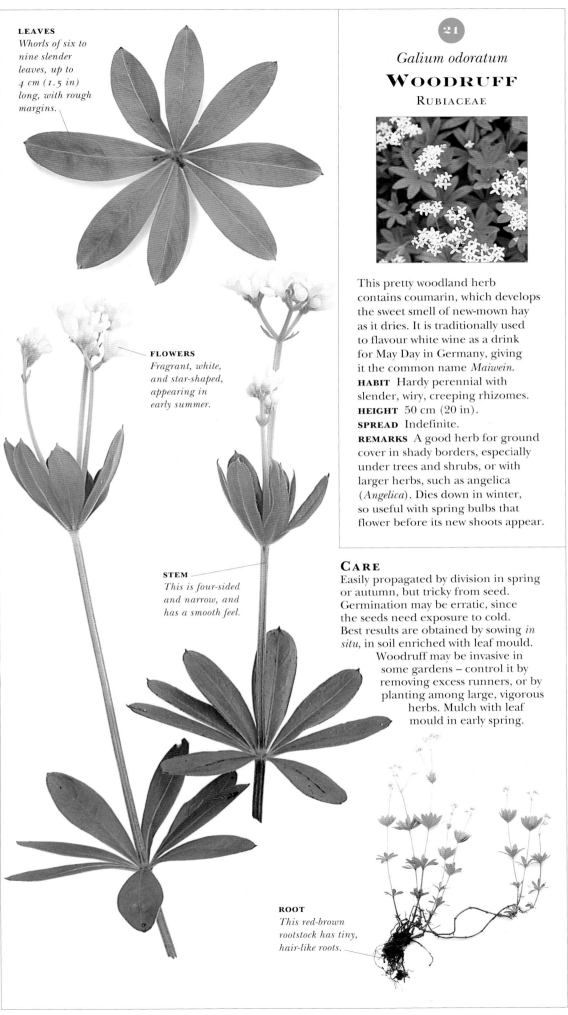

**LEAVES**
*Whorls of six to nine slender leaves, up to 4 cm (1.5 in) long, with rough margins.*

*Galium odoratum*
# WOODRUFF
RUBIACEAE

This pretty woodland herb contains coumarin, which develops the sweet smell of new-mown hay as it dries. It is traditionally used to flavour white wine as a drink for May Day in Germany, giving it the common name *Maiwein*.
**HABIT** Hardy perennial with slender, wiry, creeping rhizomes.
**HEIGHT** 50 cm (20 in).
**SPREAD** Indefinite.
**REMARKS** A good herb for ground cover in shady borders, especially under trees and shrubs, or with larger herbs, such as angelica (*Angelica*). Dies down in winter, so useful with spring bulbs that flower before its new shoots appear.

**FLOWERS**
*Fragrant, white, and star-shaped, appearing in early summer.*

## CARE
Easily propagated by division in spring or autumn, but tricky from seed. Germination may be erratic, since the seeds need exposure to cold. Best results are obtained by sowing *in situ*, in soil enriched with leaf mould. Woodruff may be invasive in some gardens – control it by removing excess runners, or by planting among large, vigorous herbs. Mulch with leaf mould in early spring.

**STEM**
*This is four-sided and narrow, and has a smooth feel.*

**ROOT**
*This red-brown rootstock has tiny, hair-like roots.*

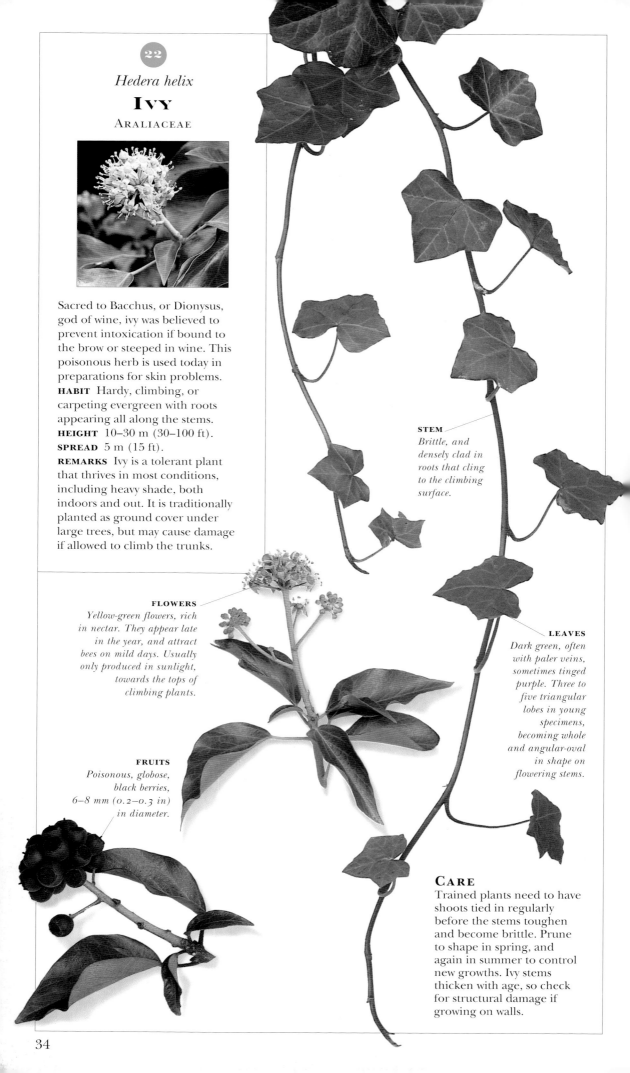

### 22

*Hedera helix*
# IVY
### ARALIACEAE

Sacred to Bacchus, or Dionysus, god of wine, ivy was believed to prevent intoxication if bound to the brow or steeped in wine. This poisonous herb is used today in preparations for skin problems.

**HABIT** Hardy, climbing, or carpeting evergreen with roots appearing all along the stems.

**HEIGHT** 10–30 m (30–100 ft).

**SPREAD** 5 m (15 ft).

**REMARKS** Ivy is a tolerant plant that thrives in most conditions, including heavy shade, both indoors and out. It is traditionally planted as ground cover under large trees, but may cause damage if allowed to climb the trunks.

**STEM**
*Brittle, and densely clad in roots that cling to the climbing surface.*

**FLOWERS**
*Yellow-green flowers, rich in nectar. They appear late in the year, and attract bees on mild days. Usually only produced in sunlight, towards the tops of climbing plants.*

**LEAVES**
*Dark green, often with paler veins, sometimes tinged purple. Three to five triangular lobes in young specimens, becoming whole and angular-oval in shape on flowering stems.*

**FRUITS**
*Poisonous, globose, black berries, 6–8 mm (0.2–0.3 in) in diameter.*

## CARE
Trained plants need to have shoots tied in regularly before the stems toughen and become brittle. Prune to shape in spring, and again in summer to control new growths. Ivy stems thicken with age, so check for structural damage if growing on walls.

**SEEDS**
*The shells are commonly striped grey-black and white, and contain kernels rich in protein, oil, vitamins, and minerals.*

## CARE
Sow in spring, in the open ground, thinning to 30–45 cm (12–18 in) apart, or in pots, planting out when about 15 cm (6 in) high. Stake plants, using stout canes or poles, before flowers develop.

**SEED HEAD**
*The seeds are edible and are arranged in concentric spirals.*

*Helianthus annuus*
# SUNFLOWER
COMPOSITAE

This cheerful, familiar garden annual is grown commercially for its edible seeds. It is an important source of polyunsaturated oil, and is also used in aromatherapy.

**HABIT** Tall, giant, hardy annual with stout stems and rough leaves. Large, daisy-like flowers in summer.
**HEIGHT** 3 m (10 ft) or more.
**SPREAD** 30–45 cm (12–18 in).
**REMARKS** Sunflowers turn to face the sun, so consider direction when planting them. They are especially effective in groups against a wall or fence, which helps protect against wind, or at the back of a border. Seeds may not ripen in areas with cold, damp autumns.

**LEAVES**
*Alternately arranged, heart-shaped, 10–30 cm (4–12 in) long and 10–20 cm (4–8 in) wide, with toothed margins and a rough texture.*

**FLOWERS**
*Large, drooping, up to 30 cm (12 in) across, with brown disc florets and yellow ray florets.*

**STEM**
*Stout, erect, usually unbranched, and hairy.*

## *Helichrysum italicum*
# CURRY PLANT
### COMPOSITAE

This silver-leaved herb fills the air
with an intriguing smell of curry,
especially after rain. The leaves
have a bitter flavour and cannot
be used to make curries, but may
be added in very small amounts
to soups and stews.

**HABIT** Evergreen, frost-hardy
subshrub with clusters of button
flowers in summer.

**HEIGHT** 60 cm (2 ft).

**SPREAD** 1 m (3 ft).

**REMARKS** Grow as a low, informal
hedge in the herb garden, or plant
at the foot of tall, woolly mullein
(*Verbascum thapsus*). Flower heads
dry well for floral arrangements
and pot-pourris.

**FLOWERS**
*Mustard-yellow and
curry-scented. Formed in
broad clusters, 2.5–5 cm
(1–2 in) across, on long,
upright, silvery stalks.*

### VARIATION

***H. i.* SUBSP.
*microphyllum***
Useful for the rock garden,
edges, and containers.
Height 25 cm (10 in).
Spread 15 cm (6 in).

## CARE
Dislikes cold, wet winters, so plant
in a sunny, sheltered position, with
good drainage. In severe winters,
protect with a layer of insulating
material. Cut back hard to old
wood in spring, since curry
plants often look bedraggled
by the end of winter.

**LEAVES**
*Long, silver-grey,
and needle-like.*

**STEM**
*White-felted
shoots, which
are woody at
the base.*

## CARE

Avoid planting next to paths and seats, since rough stems may be a hazard. Remove dead stems in winter. Mulch with well-rotted manure or compost in spring, and tie in new growths regularly. Propagate only by division or cuttings of female plants, since males are less ornamental and useful. Branches of female flowers dry well for decorations and arrangements.

**STEM**
*Climbing, twining clockwise, and bristly. It may cause abrasion or irritation to skin.*

**FLOWERS**
*Tiny, with males in clusters, and females in cone-like spikes (strobiles) which have a resinous scent.*

*Humulus lupulus*
# HOP
### CANNABIDACEAE

This hedgerow climber was first used in brewing in about the 9th century. The flavour of beer is derived from the female flowers, which also have a sedative effect.
**HABIT** Vigorous, hardy climber with deeply lobed leaves. Male and female flowers are borne on separate plants in summer.
**HEIGHT** 3–6 m (10–20 ft).
**SPREAD** 3–6 m (10–20 ft).
**REMARKS** Makes an ornamental curtain of foliage as background for the herb garden, covering fences and walls within a season. Dies down completely in winter. May also be grown over arches and pergolas to give height.

## VARIATION

**H. l. 'AUREUS' (GOLDEN HOP)**
This varation has green foliage and does not scorch in the sun. Height and spread 3–6 m (10–20 ft).

**STROBILE**
*The flowers on the female plant are found under soft, papery leaves in a strobile such as this.*

**LEAVES**
*Long-stalked, broadly heart-shaped, 10–15 cm (4–6 in) across, with three to five lobes, and coarsely toothed margins.*

## *Hyssopus officinalis*
# HYSSOP
LABIATAE

This is an old herb, mentioned in the Old Testament for its use in purification, and used by herbalists to treat bronchial infections. Its name comes from the Hebrew word *ezob*, meaning holy herb.

**HABIT** Hardy, semi-evergreen perennial with aromatic leaves. Spikes of flowers are produced in late summer.

**HEIGHT** 45–60 cm (18–24 in).

**SPREAD** 60 cm–1 m (2–3 ft).

**REMARKS** One of the best late-flowering herbs for borders, attracting bees and butterflies to its nectar-rich flowers. It may also be grown as a low hedge in knot gardens, or as edging.

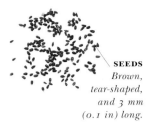

**SEEDS**
*Brown, tear-shaped, and 3 mm (0.1 in) long.*

## CARE
Trim hedges lightly, and cut back specimen plants hard in spring. To make a hedge, set young plants 23–30 cm (9–12 in) apart in spring, and pinch out the growing tips to encourage bushiness.

**LEAVES**
*Narrow, almost blunt, and up to 2.5 cm (1 in) in length. They have a bitter, sage-mint aroma.*

**FLOWERS**
*Whorls of tubular, two-lipped, purple-blue flowers, with narrow, tapering bracts.*

**H. o. 'ALBUS'**
The white-flowered hyssop is lovely in white borders. Height 45–60 cm (18–24 in). Spread 60 cm–1 m (2–3 ft).

**H.o. FORMA *roseus***
The pink-flowered form of hyssop combines well with grey-leaved artemisias. Height 45–60 cm (18–24 in). Spread 60 cm–1 m (2–3 ft).

**H. o. 'NETHERFIELD'**
A new variety, with gold-variegated foliage. Height 45 cm (18 in). Spread 60 cm (2 ft).

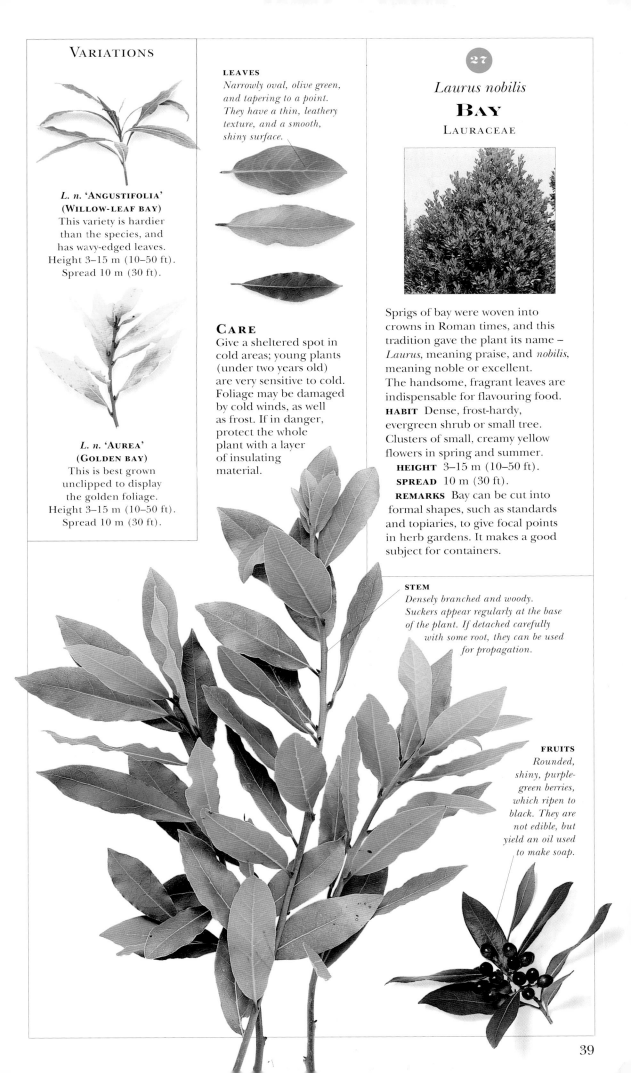

## VARIATIONS

**L. n. 'ANGUSTIFOLIA'**
**(WILLOW-LEAF BAY)**
This variety is hardier
than the species, and
has wavy-edged leaves.
Height 3–15 m (10–50 ft).
Spread 10 m (30 ft).

**L. n. 'AUREA'**
**(GOLDEN BAY)**
This is best grown
unclipped to display
the golden foliage.
Height 3–15 m (10–50 ft).
Spread 10 m (30 ft).

**LEAVES**
*Narrowly oval, olive green,
and tapering to a point.
They have a thin, leathery
texture, and a smooth,
shiny surface.*

### CARE
Give a sheltered spot in
cold areas; young plants
(under two years old)
are very sensitive to cold.
Foliage may be damaged
by cold winds, as well
as frost. If in danger,
protect the whole
plant with a layer
of insulating
material.

## *Laurus nobilis*
# BAY
### LAURACEAE

Sprigs of bay were woven into
crowns in Roman times, and this
tradition gave the plant its name –
*Laurus*, meaning praise, and *nobilis*,
meaning noble or excellent.
The handsome, fragrant leaves are
indispensable for flavouring food.
**HABIT** Dense, frost-hardy,
evergreen shrub or small tree.
Clusters of small, creamy yellow
flowers in spring and summer.
  **HEIGHT** 3–15 m (10–50 ft).
  **SPREAD** 10 m (30 ft).
  **REMARKS** Bay can be cut into
formal shapes, such as standards
and topiaries, to give focal points
in herb gardens. It makes a good
subject for containers.

**STEM**
*Densely branched and woody.
Suckers appear regularly at the base
of the plant. If detached carefully
with some root, they can be used
for propagation.*

**FRUITS**
*Rounded,
shiny, purple-
green berries,
which ripen to
black. They are
not edible, but
yield an oil used
to make soap.*

*Lavandula angustifolia*
# LAVENDER
LABIATAE

No herb garden is complete
without lavenders, with their subtle
colours and invigorating fragrance.
**HABIT** Small, evergreen shrub with
narrow, woolly, grey-green leaves
and a distinctive fragrance. Spikes
of small, purple flowers are borne
on long stalks in summer.
**HEIGHT** 60 cm–1 m (2–3 ft).
**SPREAD** 60 cm–1 m (2–3 ft).
**REMARKS** This lavender and its
many varieties are effective as dwarf,
informal hedges, and in borders,
having a neat, rounded habit.
To make a hedge, plant 23–30 cm
(9–12 in) apart in early autumn or
spring, pinching out growing tips
to encourage bushiness.

**L. a. 'HIDCOTE'**
One of the best varieties for
hedging, with a compact,
erect habit. Leaves are neat,
grey, and strongly scented,
with deep purple flowers
in dense spikes up to
5 cm (2 in) long.
Height 30–60 cm (1–2 ft).
Spread 30 cm (12 in).

**L. a.
'ROSEA'**
The classic pink lavender.
Later varieties, such as
'Loddon Pink' and 'Jean
Davis', are virtually
indistinguishable in flower
colour, habit, and perfume.
Height 23–45 cm (9–18 in).
Spread 30–45 cm (12–18 in).

**L. 'SAWYER'S'**
A hybrid lavender that
forms a distinctively broad,
dome-shaped bush, with grey
leaves and large, lavender-
blue spikes, opening
to purple. Suitable for
hedging or as a specimen
plant. Height
45–68 cm
(18–27 in).
Spread 1.1 m
(3.5 ft).

**L. a. 'NANA ALBA'**
**(DWARF WHITE LAVENDER)**
This tiny, compact lavender
has an upright habit, silver-
grey leaves, and white
flowers. It is ideal for rock
gardens, containers, white
borders, and edging, or for
a miniature hedge.
Height 15–30 cm (6–12 in).
Spread 15–45 cm (6–18 in).

**L. a. 'MUNSTEAD'**
A compact, early-flowering lavender,
with small leaves and strongly scented,
blue flowers. Seed-raised plants are not
recommended for hedging, because
they may not be uniform in size, habit,
or flower colour. Height 30–45 cm
(12–18 in). Spread 75 cm (30 in).

**L. lanata**
Woolly lavender
has white-felted
leaves, and spikes of
lilac flowers.
Height 60 cm (2 ft).
Spread 50 cm (20 in).

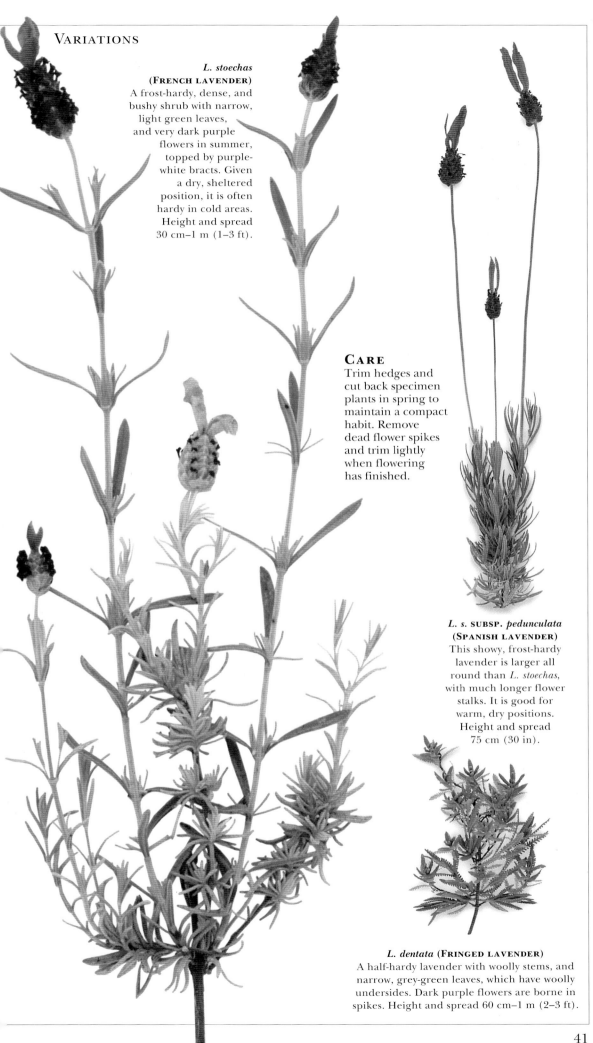

## VARIATIONS

**L. stoechas
(FRENCH LAVENDER)**
A frost-hardy, dense, and
bushy shrub with narrow,
light green leaves,
and very dark purple
flowers in summer,
topped by purple-
white bracts. Given
a dry, sheltered
position, it is often
hardy in cold areas.
Height and spread
30 cm–1 m (1–3 ft).

## CARE

Trim hedges and
cut back specimen
plants in spring to
maintain a compact
habit. Remove
dead flower spikes
and trim lightly
when flowering
has finished.

**L. s. SUBSP. *pedunculata*
(SPANISH LAVENDER)**
This showy, frost-hardy
lavender is larger all
round than *L. stoechas*,
with much longer flower
stalks. It is good for
warm, dry positions.
Height and spread
75 cm (30 in).

**L. dentata (FRINGED LAVENDER)**
A half-hardy lavender with woolly stems, and
narrow, grey-green leaves, which have woolly
undersides. Dark purple flowers are borne in
spikes. Height and spread 60 cm–1 m (2–3 ft).

## *Melissa officinalis*
# LEMON BALM
### LABIATAE

Originally grown as a bee plant, to encourage swarms into empty hives, *Melissa* gets its name from the Greek word for honeybee. It is now popular as an ingredient of herb teas and pot-pourris, because of its lemon scent and calming effects.
**HABIT** Hardy, upright perennial. Insignificant, off-white flowers appear in summer.
**HEIGHT** 30–80 cm (12–32 in).
**SPREAD** 30–45 cm (12–18 in).
**REMARKS** A useful herb for shady corners, at its best in spring before the stems elongate for flowering. Try beside the ferny leaves of sweet cicely (*Myrrhis odorata*), or reed-like chives (*Allium schoenoprasum*).

## CARE
Mulch with well-rotted manure or compost in spring. Cut back to within 15 cm (6 in) of ground level after flowering to encourage a second flush of new growth, which will remain in good condition until the first frosts. Remove dead stems just above ground level in winter.

## VARIATION

**M. o. 'AUREA'**
**(GOLDEN LEMON BALM)**
Good for damp, shady corners Height 30–40 cm (12–16 in). Spread 30–45 cm (12–18 in).

**LEAVES**
*Oval in shape, bright green, and arranged oppositely, with a slightly hairy, strongly veined surface, and neatly scalloped to toothed margins. They measure 3–8 cm (1.1–3 in) and have a delightful lemon scent, which diminishes on drying.*

**STEM**
*Erect, light green, and four-angled, branching and elongating as flower buds are formed.*

**SEEDS**
*Each seed case contains four shiny, dark brown nutlets, 1 mm (0.04 in) long. They are tear-shaped, and have white tips.*

## VARIATIONS

### M. spicata 'MOROCCAN' (MOROCCAN SPEARMINT)
A favourite culinary variety. Height 30 cm–1 m (1–3 ft). Spread indefinite.

### M. suaveolens 'VARIEGATA' (PINEAPPLE MINT)
This ornamental mint has soft, hairy leaves. Height 40 cm–1 m (16 in–3 ft). Spread indefinite.

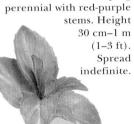

### M. aquatica (WATERMINT)
Variable, creeping perennial with red-purple stems. Height 30 cm–1 m (1–3 ft). Spread indefinite.

### M. x gracilis 'VARIEGATA' (GINGER MINT)
An attractive mint with yellow-streaked leaves, and a subtle flavour, with a hint of fruit and spice. Height 30 cm–1 m (1–3 ft). Spread indefinite.

## CARE
Mint is notoriously invasive, so plant in containers, or sink into the ground in a large pot or strong polythene bag to restrict spread. Repot annually when dormant, using rich compost and discarding all but a few short sections of rhizome. In the open ground, remove excess runners as they appear. Cut down dead stems in autumn. Mulch with well-rotted manure or compost in spring.

*Mentha spicata*

# MINT
LABIATAE

Mint is one of the oldest existing plant names. As the world's most popular flavour, it is used in many foods, drinks, and medicines.

**HABIT** Hardy, creeping perennial, whose leaves have a classic spearmint aroma. Tiny lilac to pink or white flowers are produced in a spike in summer.

**HEIGHT** 30 cm–1 m (1–3 ft).

**SPREAD** Indefinite.

**REMARKS** Plant near large, vigorous herbs that also enjoy rich, moist soil. Examples include sweet cicely (*Myrrhis odorata*) and angelica (*Angelica archangelica*). Mint flowers attract flies, so avoid planting them near seats.

**LEAVES**
*Bright green and narrowly oval, with a deeply veined surface and regularly toothed margins.*

**STEM**
*Slender, upright, and branched. It is square in cross-section.*

*Monarda didyma*
# BERGAMOT
LABIATAE

This North American woodland herb is famous as the source of Oswego tea, made by colonists to replace Indian tea following the Boston Tea Party in 1773. It has a similar aroma to the bergamot orange (*Citrus bergamia*), which is used to flavour Earl Grey tea.

**HABIT** Hardy perennial with sweetly perfumed leaves, and bright red flowers in summer and autumn.

**HEIGHT** 40 cm–1.2 m (16 in–4 ft).

**SPREAD** 30–60 cm (1–2 ft).

**REMARKS** An outstanding border plant, given suitable conditions. It is best planted in clumps of three to six, and looks good with mints (*Mentha* species).

**LEAVES**
*Oval in shape, up to 10 cm (4 in) long, and tapering to a point, with serrated margins and a reddish midrib. They have a sweet aroma, reminiscent of citrus and eau-de-cologne, which is strongest in young foliage.*

## VARIATIONS

**M. d. 'BLUE STOCKING'**
Purple-flowered, and pretty in mixed clumps. Height 1 m (3 ft). Spread 45 cm (18 in).

**M. d. 'CROFTWAY PINK'**
Try planting with mauve-flowered herbs, such as mints. Height 1 m (3 ft). Spread 45 cm (18 in).

**M. fistulosa (WILD BERGAMOT)**
Likes alkaline conditions. Height 1.2 m (4 ft). Spread 45 cm (18 in).

**FLOWERS**
*Bright red, claw-shaped, tubular flowers are produced in a single whorl, surrounded by red-green, leaf-like bracts. They attract butterflies and, in North America, humming-birds. Whole heads or individual florets can be dried for pot-pourri, retaining colour and scent well.*

**STEM**
*Squarish, light green, and hairy. It is little-branched, and tends to be red-tinged where the leaves join it.*

## CARE
Cut down dead stems in autumn. Mulch with well-rotted manure or compost in spring.

**SEEDS**
*Very large, narrowly oblong, and edible. They have a ridged, shiny surface, and are green at first, ripening to dark brown. They lack the aniseed flavour of the foliage.*

**FLOWERS**
*Tiny white flowers, produced in flat-topped clusters similar to those of cow parsley.*

## CARE
Easily grown from seed; sow outdoors in autumn, since it needs a period of cold for germination. Cut down dead foliage in autumn. Mulch with leaf mould and well-rotted manure or compost in spring. Self-sows in most gardens.

*Myrrhis odorata*

# SWEET CICELY
UMBELLIFERAE

According to John Gerard, the Elizabethan herbalist, sweet cicely "is very good for old people that are dull and without courage". The anise-scented foliage has a sweetening effect, and reduces acidity in stewed fruit.

**HABIT** Large, hardy perennial with downy, aniseed-scented leaves.
**HEIGHT** 1–2 m (3–6 ft).
**SPREAD** 60 cm–1.2 m (2–4 ft).
**REMARKS** A graceful plant for humus-rich soil, enjoying sun or shade providing conditions are moist. Use it as a foil to showier herbs, such as bergamot (*Monarda didyma*), or in a woodland border with elder (*Sambucus nigra*).

**LEAVES**
*Highly divided, fern-like, and light green. Often speckled white, with a soft texture.*

**STEM**
*Holiow, downy, and furrowed.*

## *Myrtus communis*
# MYRTLE
### MYRTACEAE

In ancient Greece and Rome, myrtle was sacred to the goddess of love, and it is carried in wedding bouquets to this day. The aromatic leaves and fruits are used in cooking in Mediterranean and Middle Eastern regions.

**HABIT** Erect, evergreen shrub, which is frost hardy to half hardy, according to position.

**HEIGHT AND SPREAD** 3 m (10 ft) in the wild, 1–1.2 m (3–4 ft) in colder areas and pots.

**REMARKS** In cold areas this shrub will need a warm, sheltered spot, preferably against a sunny wall. It also makes a lovely container plant for patios and garden rooms.

## VARIATION

**M. c. SUBSP.** *tarentina*
**'MICROPHYLLA VARIEGATA'**
A variegated myrtle with light green, cream-edged leaves. It is less hardy than the plain variety. Height 1–2 m (3–6 ft). Spread 1 m (3 ft).

**M. c. SUBSP.**
*tarentina*
This compact variety has a very dense habit, small, neat leaves, and numerous small flowers in summer, followed by white fruits. It is wind-resistant, and good for hedging in mild areas. Height 1–2 m (3–6 ft). Spread 1 m (3 ft).

## CARE
To restrict size, cut back hard in spring, and pinch out regularly. Water freely during the growing season, but keep pot plants just moist in winter. Repot in alternate years in spring, and feed fortnightly with liquid fertilizer in spring and summer. Outdoors, plant myrtles in late spring, and protect with a layer of insulating fleece during frosty weather.

**FLOWERS**
*Fragrant, white, five-petalled flowers, filled with numerous golden stamens.*

**FLOWERS**
*They are produced singly between the leaves and stem. The flowers are distilled for eau d'ange, a skin tonic dating back to the 16th century.*

**LEAVES**
*Dark, lustrous green, and oval in shape, with a juniper-like aroma. They are arranged densely along the branches.*

**STEM**
*Slender, red-brown, and woody, with a much-branched, upright habit.*

**STEM**
*Erect, branched, hairy, and square in cross-section, with the same pungent aroma as the leaves.*

**LEAVES**
*Grey-green, heart-shaped to oval, with a hairy surface, toothed margins, and a mint-thyme aroma. They dry well, and can be used for stuffing cat toys.*

## CARE
Cut back dead stems in autumn, and at any time plants look untidy. Mulch with well-rotted manure or compost in spring. Cover young plants with netting to protect them against cats until they are large enough to withstand attention. Stake mature plants in spring to minimize any damage.

**SEEDS**
*Seeds cases contain four smooth, oval, dark brown nutlets with a white mark at each end. They are viable for five years.*

*Nepeta cataria*
# CATNIP (CATMINT)
### LABIATAE

Catnip contains compounds that have a stimulant effect on cats, who chew the plant and roll in it.
**HABIT** Hardy perennial with an upright habit, and leaves with a pungent aroma. White, purple-spotted, tubular flowers are borne in summer and early autumn.
**HEIGHT** 30 cm–1 m (1–3 ft).
**SPREAD** 60 cm (2 ft).
**REMARKS** Not as attractive as garden catmints, so best at the back of a border, or where damage by cats will not matter. Grow it among tidier, more colourful herbs, such as evening primroses (*Oenothera biennis*) and opium poppies (*Papaver somniferum*).

## VARIATION

**N. racemosa**
**(SYN. N. mussinii)**
This bushy variety makes a good ornamental plant, but is less attractive to cats than *N. cataria*. Height and spread 45 cm (18 in).

*Ocimum basilicum*

# BASIL

### LABIATAE

This sweetly aromatic herb is tropical Asian in origin, but has become indispensable in Italian cooking. It is traditionally grown in Hindu homes and around temples, as a sacred plant.

**HABIT** Tender annual with an upright, branched habit.

**HEIGHT** 20–60 cm (8–24 in).

**SPREAD** 15–30 cm (6–12 in).

**REMARKS** Basil is rarely successful in the open ground in areas with cool summers, but does well in pots. Combine its lush foliage with curly parsley, or plant several varieties together. The small-leaved bush basil and purple-leaved 'Dark Opal' have distinctive, contrasting foliage.

**SEEDS**
*Seed cases contain four brown, tear-shaped nutlets.*

**LEAVES**
*Broadly oval and bright green, barely toothed, and up to 5 cm (2 in) long. They are thin in texture, and have an intense, clove-like aroma.*

**STEM**
*Light green, branched, round at the base, and becoming square in cross-section higher up.*

**FLOWERS**
*White, tubular, two-lipped flowers, 8 mm (0.3 in) long, are produced in summer in whorled spikes.*

## CARE

Basil needs ample warmth and light, so seed should not be sown until late spring, maintaining a minimum temperature of 13°C (55°F). Pot up individually, or put three in a 25 cm (10 in) pot when large enough to handle. Pots of seedlings can also be bought in supermarkets, and divided for growing on in pots. For a succession of young leaves for cutting, sow in trays at intervals of three weeks throughout the summer.

**O. b.
'CITRIODORUM'
(LEMON BASIL)**
A basil from north-
west India, with a
bushy habit, narrowly
oval leaves, and white
flowers. It has a
refreshing citrus scent.
Height 45–60 cm
(18–24 in). Spread
25–35 cm (10–14 in).

**O. b. VAR.
*crispum*
(CURLY BASIL)**
A robust basil
with large,
extravagantly ruffled
leaves, and a fine flavour. It
is often called 'Neapolitana'.
Height 20–60 cm (8–24 in).
Spread 15–45 cm (6–18 in).

**O. b. 'ANISE'**
Originally from Persia,
this variety has distinctive
purple stems, purple-veined
leaves, and light pink
flowers. It has a sweet,
anise-liquorice aroma, and
is sometimes called 'Licorice'. Height
45 cm (18 in). Spread 30 cm (12 in).

**O. b. VAR.
*minimum*
(BUSH BASIL,
GREEK BASIL)**
This dwarf,
compact variety is
hardier than the species.
It has very small leaves, less
than 1 cm (0.4 in) long, and a
reasonably good flavour. It makes
a neat plant for pots. Height and
spread 15–30 cm (6–12 in).

**O. b.
'DARK OPAL'
('PURPUREUM')**
An attractive
variety with
deep purple-
black leaves,
and cerise-pink
flowers. Plant with
mixed culinary, or
grey-leaved, herbs.
Height 60 cm (2 ft).
Spread 30 cm (12 in).

**O. b. 'PURPLE
RUFFLES'**
This variety is
similar to 'Dark Opal',
but with ruffled, deeply
toothed leaves. It makes a
splendid specimen plant for
containers. Height and spread
45–60 cm (18–24 in).

49

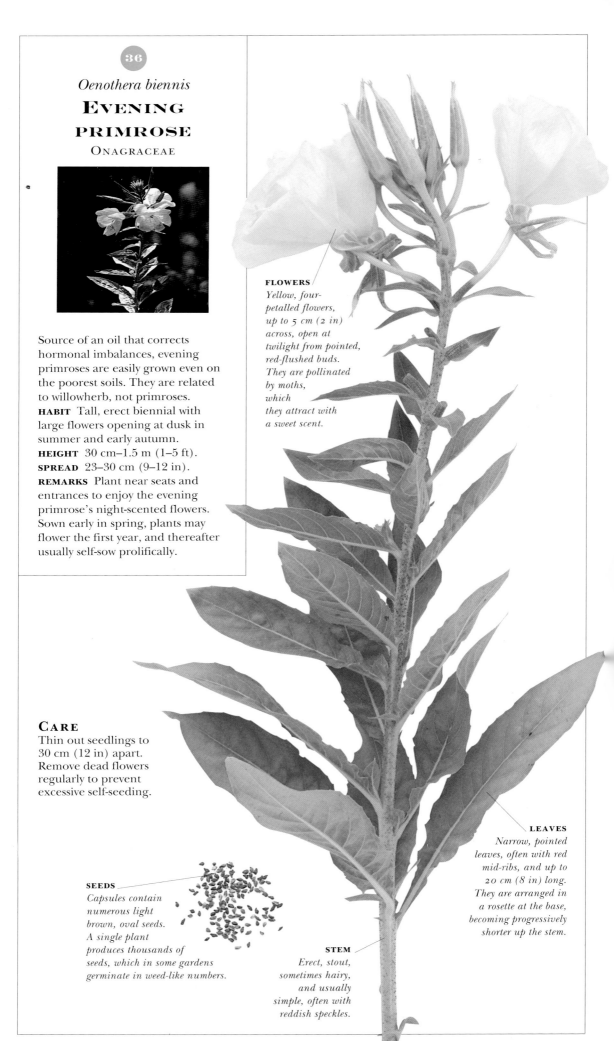

**36**

*Oenothera biennis*

# EVENING PRIMROSE

ONAGRACEAE

Source of an oil that corrects hormonal imbalances, evening primroses are easily grown even on the poorest soils. They are related to willowherb, not primroses.

**HABIT** Tall, erect biennial with large flowers opening at dusk in summer and early autumn.

**HEIGHT** 30 cm–1.5 m (1–5 ft).

**SPREAD** 23–30 cm (9–12 in).

**REMARKS** Plant near seats and entrances to enjoy the evening primrose's night-scented flowers. Sown early in spring, plants may flower the first year, and thereafter usually self-sow prolifically.

**FLOWERS**
*Yellow, four-petalled flowers, up to 5 cm (2 in) across, open at twilight from pointed, red-flushed buds. They are pollinated by moths, which they attract with a sweet scent.*

**CARE**
Thin out seedlings to 30 cm (12 in) apart. Remove dead flowers regularly to prevent excessive self-seeding.

**SEEDS**
*Capsules contain numerous light brown, oval seeds. A single plant produces thousands of seeds, which in some gardens germinate in weed-like numbers.*

**LEAVES**
*Narrow, pointed leaves, often with red mid-ribs, and up to 20 cm (8 in) long. They are arranged in a rosette at the base, becoming progressively shorter up the stem.*

**STEM**
*Erect, stout, sometimes hairy, and usually simple, often with reddish speckles.*

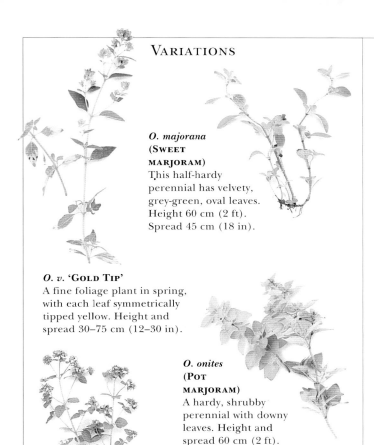

**O. majorana (SWEET MARJORAM)**
This half-hardy perennial has velvety, grey-green, oval leaves. Height 60 cm (2 ft). Spread 45 cm (18 in).

**O. v. 'GOLD TIP'**
A fine foliage plant in spring, with each leaf symmetrically tipped yellow. Height and spread 30–75 cm (12–30 in).

**O. onites (POT MARJORAM)**
A hardy, shrubby perennial with downy leaves. Height and spread 60 cm (2 ft).

**O. v. 'AUREUM'**
The most popular variety, with small, yellow-green leaves. Height and spread 75 cm (30 in).

*Origanum vulgare*

# MARJORAM & OREGANO

### LABIATAE

All marjorams have a long flowering period, and attract butterflies and bees. Plants grown in hot, dry areas have the strongest aroma.

**HABIT** Variable, hardy perennial with a bushy habit, and broadly oval, aromatic leaves.

**HEIGHT** 45 cm (18 in).

**SPREAD** 45 cm (18 in).

**REMARKS** Marjorams are subtle in colour, shape, and texture, and harmonize well with other Mediterranean herbs that enjoy sunny, warm, and dry conditions. These include thymes (*Thymus* species) and savories (*Satureja*).

**FLOWERS**
*Mauve to pink or white, bell-shaped, tubular flowers are borne in branched clusters.*

**LEAVES**
*Variable leaves, with a peppery, thyme-like aroma. They may be hairy or smooth, oval to rounded, and pointed or blunt.*

**STEM**
*More or less upright, light purple-brown, and hairy. It roots at the base.*

### CARE
Grow oregano hard for the best flavour, in the sunniest, warmest position possible. Cut back dead stems to ground level in winter. Trim after flowering to encourage a flush of new leaves.

*Papaver rhoeas*

# POPPY

PAPAVERACEAE

Poppies contain pain-killing compounds, which are extracted from the green capsules. They are also cultivated for their seeds, which are used in baking and for an almond-flavoured salad oil.

**HABIT** Hardy annual with a slender taproot and red blooms in summer.

**HEIGHT** 20–60 cm (8–24 in).

**SPREAD** 15–30 cm (6–12 in).

**REMARKS** Useful for filling gaps, or for a special area of annual herbs. To collect seed or to dry capsules for ornamental use, cut the stems before they start to turn brown, and hang upside-down over a sheet of paper. The capsules will shed seeds as the "pepperpot" opens.

**SEEDS**
*Numerous, tiny, dark brown seeds are contained in a flat-topped, tulip-shaped to rounded capsule, 1–2 cm (0.4–0.8 in) long.*

**FLOWERS**
*Bright red, four-petalled flowers, usually with a dark spot at the base of each petal, open from oval, bristly buds. They are short-lived, lasting less than a day.*

**STEM**
*Light green, upright stems, which are clad in stiff hairs.*

## CARE
Poppies do not transplant successfully. Sow seed where the plants are to flower, thinning to 30 cm (12 in) apart. To prevent excessive self-seeding, remove seed capsules as they form.

## VARIATION

**P. somniferum (OPIUM POPPY)**
Hardy annual with waxy leaves. All parts are poisonous. It is illegal to grow opium poppies of any variety in some countries. Height 65 cm–1 m (26 in–3 ft). Spread 23 cm–1 m (9 in–3 ft).

**LEAVES**
*Bright green, deeply cut and lobed, and roughly oval to narrowly oval in outline, with bristly hairs on the undersurface.*

## VARIATIONS

**P. 'PRINCE OF ORANGE'**
An orange-scented hybrid
with a compact habit, and
green, fan-shaped leaves.
Height and spread
60 cm (2 ft).

**P. citronellum**
Upright and bushy shrub,
with deeply veined leaves.
Height 30 cm–1 m (1–3 ft).
Spread 30–60 cm (1–2 ft).

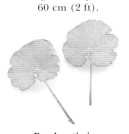

**P. odoratissimum**
**(APPLE PELARGONIUM)**
Low-growing shrub, with
light green, rounded leaves.
Height 30 cm (12 in).
Spread 60 cm (2 ft).

**P. quercifolium**
**(OAK-LEAVED PELARGONIUM)**
This upright shrub has
rough, sticky leaves.
Height 45–60 cm (18–24 in).
Spread 1 m (3 ft).

---

**39**

*Pelargonium capitatum*
## SCENTED
## PELARGONIUM
### GERANIACEAE

Southern African in origin, scented
pelargoniums have demure colours,
a wide range of aromas, and
appealing leaf shapes and textures.
**HABIT** Tender, shrubby, evergreen
perennial with sage green, crinkled
leaves, which are rose-scented.
**HEIGHT** 30–60 cm (1–2 ft).
**SPREAD** 30–45 cm (12–18 in).
**REMARKS** Grow in pots beside
seats and entrances, where you
can enjoy their scent. They can also
be used as bedding plants, to fill
gaps in the herb garden, and
in mild areas may survive outdoor
in very sunny, sheltered spots.

---

## CARE
Cut back in early spring to
remove straggly growths,
and pinch out regularly
to encourage a bushy habit.
Plants grown in the open may
be lifted and brought under
cover for the winter; they
can be cut back hard
when potting up.

**STEM**
*Hairy, green,
and quite brittle,
becoming woody
at the base.*

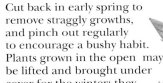

**FLOWERS**
*Mauve-pink, with purple
veining, in clusters of one
to twenty. They are about
2 cm (0.8 in) across,
which is relatively large for
a scented pelargonium.*

**LEAVES**
*Soft, green,
velvety, and crinkled,
with irregularly lobed
margins. They have a
rose scent, and are the
source of geranium oil .*

*Petroselinum crispum*

# PARSLEY

UMBELLIFERAE

Though often discarded as a garnish, parsley is one of the most beneficial herbs to include in the diet. Its leaves are rich in vitamins A and C, minerals, and compounds that clear toxins from the system.

**HABIT** Hardy biennial, usually grown as an annual, with triangular leaves. Tiny, yellow-green flowers are produced in flat-topped clusters in the summer of the second year.

**HEIGHT** 38 cm (15 in), reaching 80 cm (32 in) when flowering.

**SPREAD** 30 cm (12 in).

**REMARKS** One of the most ornamental culinary herbs. Plant it as a contrast to plain-leaved herbs such as sorrel (*Rumex acetosa*).

**SEEDS**
*Curved, oval, grey-brown, and 3 mm (0.1 in) long. They have a ridged surface, and are aromatic, with a strong parsley flavour.*

**LEAVES**
*Rich green, aromatic, and triangular in outline. Divided into diamond-shaped, toothed leaflets, which in cultivated plants have densely curled margins.*

**STEM**
*Light green, solid, and succulent, with a ribbed surface and a strong aroma.*

## VARIATION

**P. c. 'ITALIAN'
(PLAIN-LEAVED PARSLEY)**
This has dark green, flat foliage with a strong flavour. Plants have long stalks and are large and weather-resistant, making them better suited to the open ground than to containers. Height and spread 38–60 cm (15–24 in).

**ROOT**
*Thick, white-fleshed taproot with a stronger parsley flavour than stems or leaves.*

## CARE
Sow seed at intervals from late winter to early summer for a year-round supply. Seeds are slow to germinate, taking three to six weeks, unless soaked overnight in warm water before sowing. In cold areas, over-wintering plants need a sunny, sheltered position.

## VARIATIONS

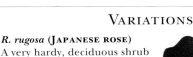

### R. rugosa (JAPANESE ROSE)
A very hardy, deciduous shrub with dense, prickly stems, dark green leaves which turn yellow in autumn, and scented, single, purple-pink (or pink, or white) flowers in summer. This makes an excellent hedge.

### R. gallica 'VERSICOLOR' (ROSA MUNDI)
This variety has a similar habit to the Apothecary's rose, and bears semi-double, slightly scented flowers, which are pale pink, with deep pink stripes. Height 75 cm (30 in). Spread 1 m (3 ft).

### R. g. VAR. officinalis (APOTHECARY'S ROSE)
A neat, bushy, deciduous shrub, with bristly stems and leathery leaves. The flowers are pink.

## 41

### Rosa canina
# WILD ROSE
ROSACEAE

Roses have long been important in skin products, perfumery, medicine, and food flavouring. The wild rose is the heraldic emblem of England, and the origin of the "English rose" complexion.
**HABIT** Hardy, deciduous shrub with pink to white, scented flowers in summer, followed by scarlet hips.
**HEIGHT** 3 m (10 ft).
**SPREAD** 3 m (10 ft).
**REMARKS** Rather rampant for general garden use, but if space allows, plant in collections of wildflowers or native herbs. Train on a frame to control arching stems. It can also be incorporated into large, informal hedges.

## CARE
Remove dead or damaged stems, and weak growths in early winter. Wild roses flower on the previous year's growth, and should not be cut back hard.

**FLOWERS**
*Pink to white, fragrant, five-petalled flowers produced in clusters of up to four in summer. They are single and short-lived.*

**LEAVES**
*Mid-green, smooth, and mostly divided into five or seven oval, toothed leaflets.*

**PETALS**
*These keep their scent if dried and can be used for pot-pourris.*

**FRUITS**
*Bright red, shiny, egg-shaped hips, which ripen in autumn.*

**STEM**
*Vigorous, arching, and green, climbing by means of stout, downwards curving thorns.*

## 42

*Rosmarinus officinalis*

# ROSEMARY

LABIATAE

Rosemary symbolizes friendship, loyalty, and remembrance. Its name means "dew of the sea" – it grows wild on the coast, and the pale blue flowers can look like dew.

**HABIT** Variable, evergreen shrub, with an upright to spreading habit. It is considered frost hardy, but plants vary in hardiness according to origin, age, and conditions.

**HEIGHT** 2 m (6 ft).

**SPREAD** 1.5–2 m (5–6 ft).

**REMARKS** This decorative shrub makes an excellent container plant, and also thrives in dry conditions on steep banks and gravel drives. It is a good contrast to larger leaved, evergreen herbs.

**LEAVES**
*Leathery, tough, and needle-like, with blunt ends. They have a dark green upper surface, pale downy underside, and a strong, resinous scent.*

**SEEDS**
*Seed cases contain four small, smooth, light brown nutlets.*

**STEM**
*Upright to spreading, brown, woody branches, with mostly four-angled stems. Branches are brittle, breaking easily under snow.*

**FLOWERS**
*Borne in small clusters in spring in the leaf axils. Individual flowers are ice blue, tubular, and two-lipped, with the lower lip much larger and three-lobed.*

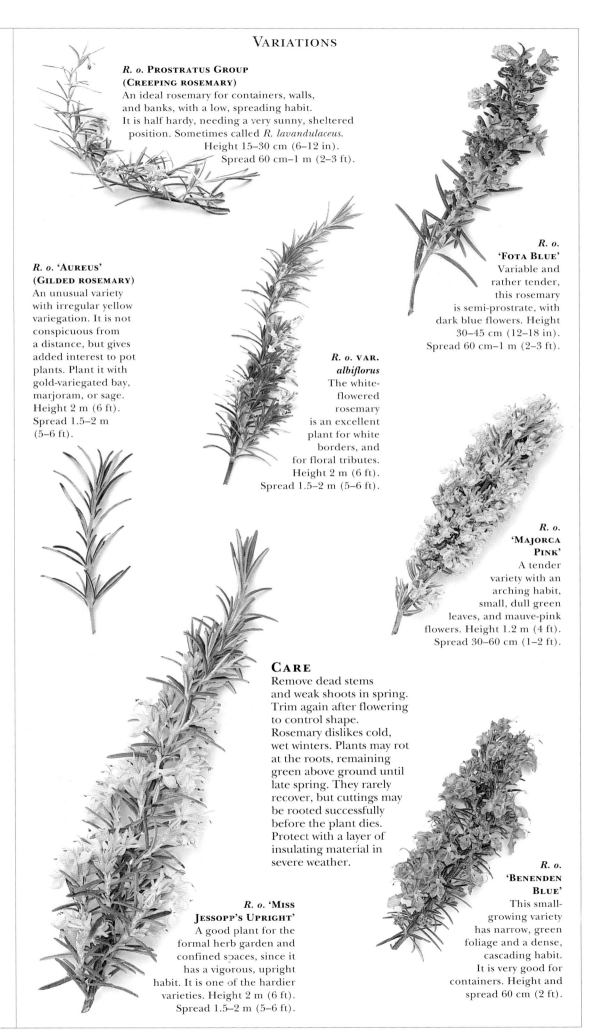

# VARIATIONS

### R. o. PROSTRATUS GROUP (CREEPING ROSEMARY)
An ideal rosemary for containers, walls, and banks, with a low, spreading habit. It is half hardy, needing a very sunny, sheltered position. Sometimes called *R. lavandulaceus*. Height 15–30 cm (6–12 in). Spread 60 cm–1 m (2–3 ft).

### R. o. 'FOTA BLUE'
Variable and rather tender, this rosemary is semi-prostrate, with dark blue flowers. Height 30–45 cm (12–18 in). Spread 60 cm–1 m (2–3 ft).

### R. o. 'AUREUS' (GILDED ROSEMARY)
An unusual variety with irregular yellow variegation. It is not conspicuous from a distance, but gives added interest to pot plants. Plant it with gold-variegated bay, marjoram, or sage. Height 2 m (6 ft). Spread 1.5–2 m (5–6 ft).

### R. o. VAR. albiflorus
The white-flowered rosemary is an excellent plant for white borders, and for floral tributes. Height 2 m (6 ft). Spread 1.5–2 m (5–6 ft).

### R. o. 'MAJORCA PINK'
A tender variety with an arching habit, small, dull green leaves, and mauve-pink flowers. Height 1.2 m (4 ft). Spread 30–60 cm (1–2 ft).

## CARE
Remove dead stems and weak shoots in spring. Trim again after flowering to control shape. Rosemary dislikes cold, wet winters. Plants may rot at the roots, remaining green above ground until late spring. They rarely recover, but cuttings may be rooted successfully before the plant dies. Protect with a layer of insulating material in severe weather.

### R. o. 'BENENDEN BLUE'
This small-growing variety has narrow, green foliage and a dense, cascading habit. It is very good for containers. Height and spread 60 cm (2 ft).

### R. o. 'MISS JESSOPP'S UPRIGHT'
A good plant for the formal herb garden and confined spaces, since it has a vigorous, upright habit. It is one of the hardier varieties. Height 2 m (6 ft). Spread 1.5–2 m (5–6 ft).

## *Rumex acetosa*
# SORREL
POLYGONACEAE

Popular since at least Roman times as a pot herb, sorrel comes somewhere between a herb and a vegetable. Though too astringent to eat in the same quantities as spinach, its acidic flavour is pleasant in salads and soups.
**HABIT** Hardy perennial with dock-like leaves and tall spikes of reddish green flowers in summer.
**HEIGHT** 50 cm–1 m (20–36 in).
**SPREAD** 25–45 cm (10–18 in).
**REMARKS** Sorrel's simple, broad leaves provide a contrast to the foliage of curly parsley (*Petroselinum crispum*) and wild strawberry (*Fragaria vesca*). The leaves become more astringent as they age.

# VARIATIONS

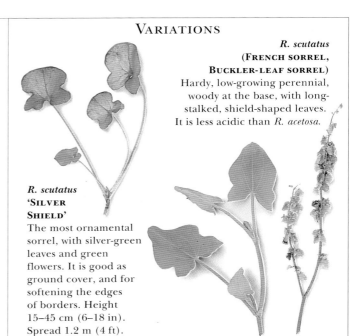

**R. scutatus 'SILVER SHIELD'**
The most ornamental sorrel, with silver-green leaves and green flowers. It is good as ground cover, and for softening the edges of borders. Height 15–45 cm (6–18 in). Spread 1.2 m (4 ft).

***R. scutatus* (FRENCH SORREL, BUCKLER-LEAF SORREL)**
Hardy, low-growing perennial, woody at the base, with long-stalked, shield-shaped leaves. It is less acidic than *R. acetosa*.

**LEAVES**
*Broad, oblong, and bright green, with a long stalk and arrow-shaped base. Lower leaves are up to 15 cm (6 in) long, becoming smaller, with shorter stalks, higher up the stem.*

**SEEDS**
*Small, brown, shiny, pointed, and three-sided.*

# CARE
For a long period of leaf production remove flower spikes as they appear. For winter supply, cover plants with cloches or keep pots of sorrel frost-free under glass.

**STEM**
*Red-tinged and juicy, with a ridged surface.*

## SEEDS
*Capsules with four or five lobes split open when ripe, shedding tiny black seeds.*

## FLOWERS
*Mustard yellow flowers, with four fringed petals, are borne in open clusters in summer.*

## LEAVES
*Blue-green and deeply divided, with club-shaped lobes and an aroma resembling wet paint.*

## *Ruta graveolens*
# RUE
RUTACEAE

Rue was once renowned as an antidote to poisons and infectious diseases. It also had a reputation for improving eyesight, and was used by Renaissance artists.

**HABIT** Hardy, evergreen subshrub with pungently aromatic leaves.

**HEIGHT** 60 cm (2 ft).

**SPREAD** 45 cm (18 in).

**REMARKS** One of the best shrubs for confined spaces, with a dense, compact habit and neat foliage that remains in good condition all year. For winter effect, plant next to purple sage (*Salvia officinalis* 'Purpurascens'); and in summer, try it beside pink bergamot (*Monarda* 'Croftway Pink').

## VARIATIONS

**R. g. 'JACKMAN'S BLUE'**
An outstanding foliage plant, with steely blue leaves. Height 60 cm (2 ft). Spread 45 cm (18 in).

## CARE
Prune hard in spring to maintain compact shape, but do not cut into main stem. Wear gloves since it contains compounds that can cause severe skin irritation.

## STEM
*Blue-green, and becoming woody at the base.*

**R. g. 'VARIEGATA'**
This variety has irregular cream variegation, and the occasional entirely white leaf. Height 60 cm (2 ft). Spread 45 cm (18 in).

*Salvia officinalis*

# SAGE

LABIATAE

Sage has long been revered as a longevity herb. It is also one of the most widely used culinary herbs, and an excellent garden plant.

**HABIT** Hardy, evergreen shrub with aromatic leaves and spikes of purple-blue, two-lipped flowers.

**HEIGHT** 60–80 cm (24–32 in).

**SPREAD** 1 m (3 ft).

**REMARKS** The soft colour and texture of sage is a perfect foil for the spiky leaves of rosemary (*Rosmarinus officinalis*) and thyme (*Thymus* species). Its simple foliage is also effective with the finely cut leaves of artemisias (*Artemisia* species), and makes a good contrast to dark, glossy evergreens.

## VARIATIONS

**S.o. 'PURPURASCENS' (PURPLE SAGE)**
This sage has purple-grey, velvety leaves. Height 60–80 cm (24–32 in). Spread 1 m (3 ft).

**S.o. 'KEW GOLD'**
A pretty sage with yellow foliage and a compact habit. It is especially effective with yellow- and orange-flowered herbs. Height 30 cm (12 in). Spread 45 cm (18 in).

**S. sclarea (CLARY SAGE)**
A fast-growing, tall biennial with aromatic, oval leaves, and spikes of flowers. Height 1m (3 ft). Spread 60 cm (2 ft).

**S.o. 'ICTERINA'**
The yellow-variegated leaves of this variety can be used to add interest to the plain greens of parsley, bay, and chives. Height 60–80 cm (24–32 in). Spread 1 m (3 ft).

**LEAVES**
*Oval, pointed, and pale grey-green, with a velvety surface.*

**STEM**
*Much-branched, four-angled, and finely downy, becoming woody at the base.*

## CARE

Sage bushes tend to become woody and sparse with age, so aim to replace plants after their fourth or fifth year. They are easily propagated from cuttings. Variants will not come true from seed.

## VARIATION

**S. n. 'GUINCHO PURPLE'
(PURPLE ELDER)**
This variety has dark
purple-bronze foliage
and pink-stamened,
cream flowers. Height
and spread 6 m (20 ft).

## CARE
Elder comes into leaf
very early in the year, so
prune hard in late winter
before the buds swell.
If grown for its foliage,
rather than for flowers
and fruits, cut back to
within 30 cm (12 in) of
ground level, which will
encourage strong new
shoots from the base.

**STEM**
*Arching stems have
corky, grey-brown bark.
They are brittle, and when
broken have the same foetid
smell as the leaves.*

## *Sambucus nigra*
# ELDER
### CAPRIFOLIACEAE

Elder has provided remedies for
most common complaints, from
colds and flu to skin problems.
Elderflower water remains popular
in cosmetics, and both flowers and
berries make country wines.
**HABIT** Hardy, deciduous, shrubby
tree with attractive flowers.
**HEIGHT** 4.5–10 m (15–30 ft).
**SPREAD** 4–4.5 m (12–15 ft).
**REMARKS** Though the varieties are
more ornamental as garden shrubs,
common elder is a good subject
for informal hedges and wildflower
gardens. Plant it as a background
for other woodland herbs, such as
sweet cicely (*Myrrhis odorata*) and
foxgloves (*Digitalis purpurea*).

**FLOWERS**
*Cream flowers, 5 mm
(0.2 in) across, are
produced in flat-topped
clusters, 10–20 cm
(4–8 in) across, in
early summer. Their
scent has been likened
to muscatel wine.*

**LEAVES**
*Divided into five to
seven oval leaflets, and
tapering towards the tip.
Elder leaves may turn
bronze, cream, and
pink in autumn.*

61

# *Santolina chamaecyparissus*
## COTTON LAVENDER
### COMPOSITAE

Grown by the ancient Greeks and Romans, cotton lavender became popular in northern Europe during the 16th century as a knot-garden plant. Its foliage repels insects.

**HABIT** Hardy, aromatic, evergreen shrub with narrow grey leaves.

**HEIGHT** 20–50 cm (8–20 in).

**SPREAD** 60 cm (2 ft).

**REMARKS** The neat, silver-grey foliage of cotton lavender makes an excellent dwarf hedge. In a knot-garden it will provide contrast to dark green hedging plants, such as box (*Buxus sempervirens* 'Suffruticosa').

**LEAVES**
*Narrow, silver-grey, and woolly. They are finely divided into closely packed, blunt segments, and have a pungent aroma.*

**CARE**
To make a hedge, set young plants 30–38 cm (12–15 in) apart in spring, and pinch out growing points to encourage a bushy habit. Prune twice a year, in spring and again after flowering. Trim lightly to shape several times during the growing season.

**FLOWERS**
*Solitary heads of tightly packed, tubular florets, deep yellow in colour, are produced on slender grey stalks. They are long-lasting.*

**STEM**
*Grey-green and woolly, becoming brown and woody at the base.*

## VARIATIONS

**S. c. 'LEMON QUEEN'**
This variety has cream flowers. Height 25–40cm (10–16 in). Spread 30–50 cm (12–20 in).

**S. pinnata SUBSP. neapolitana**
A rounded shrub with grey-green, woolly leaves. Height 75 cm (30 in). Spread 1 m (3 ft).

**S. rosmarinifolia (SYN. S. virens) (HOLY FLAX)**
Unlike most cotton lavenders, this kind has bright green leaves. Yellow flowers appear in summer. Height 60 cm (2 ft). Spread 1 m (3 ft).

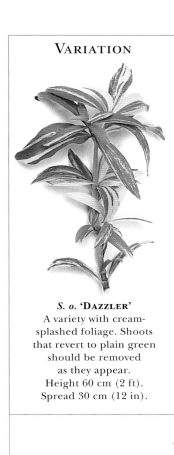

**FLOWERS**
*Clusters of scented
flowers, about
2.5 cm (1 in)
across, resembling
small pinks.*

**S. o. 'DAZZLER'**
A variety with cream-
splashed foliage. Shoots
that revert to plain green
should be removed
as they appear.
Height 60 cm (2 ft).
Spread 30 cm (12 in).

*Saponaria officinalis*
# SOAPWORT
CARYOPHYLLACEAE

Before commercial soap production
began in the 1800s, soapwort was
grown in cottage gardens to make
soap suds for washing. It is long-
lived, often found in derelict
gardens, and late-flowering – hence
the name "goodbye-to-summer".
**HABIT** Hardy perennial with
creeping rhizomes and broadly
oval, pointed leaves.
**HEIGHT** 30 cm–1 m (1–3 ft).
**SPREAD** 60 cm (2 ft).
**REMARKS** A vigorous perennial
for the border. Its flowers look
pretty against dark plants, such
as purple elder (*Sambucus nigra*
'Guincho Purple'), or with the
mauve spikes of flowering mints.

## CARE
Stake in early summer
to prevent flopping
as flower heads develop.
Tends to be invasive, so
divide each year, or plant
near other large, vigorous
herbs. Cut back dead
stems in winter. Do not
plant where roots or
foliage may contact pond
water, since soapwort
is poisonous to fish.

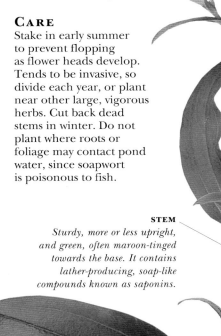

**FLOWERS**
*Usually pale pink and
single in the wild, but
double-flowered and
rose-pink varieties are
common in gardens.*

**STEM**
*Sturdy, more or less upright,
and green, often maroon-tinged
towards the base. It contains
lather-producing, soap-like
compounds known as saponins.*

**LEAVES**
*Broadly oval and
pointed, with three
distinct, parallel
main veins.*

## *Satureja montana*
# WINTER SAVORY
### LABIATAE

Winter savory has a stronger flavour than summer savory, and can be picked fresh from the garden all year round, even in winter. Savory is known as "the bean herb", since its peppery, thyme-like aroma has an affinity with pulses of all kinds.

**HABIT** Hardy, shrubby perennial with small, narrow, evergreen leaves, which are strongly aromatic.

**HEIGHT** 38 cm (15 in).

**SPREAD** 20 cm (8 in).

**REMARKS** Winter savory is a typical Mediterranean herb, thriving on sun-baked, stony hillsides. Grow it with thyme (*Thymus* species) or marjoram (*Origanum* species), or plant as a dwarf, informal hedge.

## VARIATIONS

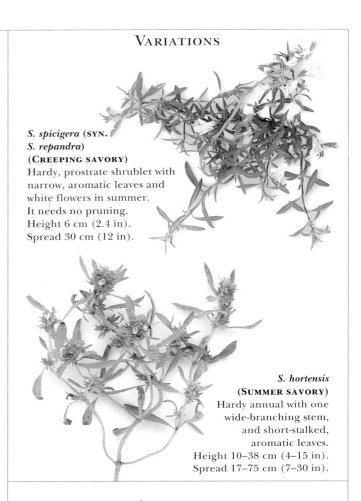

*S. spicigera* (SYN. *S. repandra*) (**CREEPING SAVORY**)
Hardy, prostrate shrublet with narrow, aromatic leaves and white flowers in summer. It needs no pruning.
Height 6 cm (2.4 in).
Spread 30 cm (12 in).

*S. hortensis* (**SUMMER SAVORY**)
Hardy annual with one wide-branching stem, and short-stalked, aromatic leaves.
Height 10–38 cm (4–15 in).
Spread 17–75 cm (7–30 in).

**LEAVES**
*Stalkless, narrow, pointed, and up to 3 cm (1.1 in) long. They are strongly aromatic, with a spicy, thyme-like aroma.*

**FLOWERS**
*Small, white to pale pink or purple flowers in whorls of up to fourteen. The petals are fused into a two-lipped tube, typical for the* Labiatae *family.*

**STEM**
*Smooth to minutely hairy stems, becoming woody at the base.*

**CARE**
For hedges, plant 23 cm (9 in) apart, and pinch out to encourage bushy growth. Prune established plants in spring and autumn. Grow hard, since feeding with nitrogen-rich manure produces weak growth.

## VARIATION

**S. t. 'ROYAL RUBY'**
One of several varieties with a pronounced deep maroon flush, especially towards the centre of the rosette. Grow it as a contrast to the green varieties. It does not come true from seed.

**50**

*Sempervivum tectorum*
# HOUSELEEK
CRASSULACEAE

Grown in ornamental containers in front of houses during Roman times, and traditionally planted on roofs as a protection against lightning, houseleeks are one of the earliest recorded "houseplants".
**HABIT** Hardy, evergreen, succulent perennial. Each rosette of fleshy leaves produces several smaller rosettes before flowering and dying, forming a large clump.
**HEIGHT** 5–8 cm (2–3 in).
**SPREAD** 30 cm (12 in).
**REMARKS** A trouble-free herb that remains neat and attractive all year round. Plant in pots, or in the crevices of walls and paving slabs, and at the edges of paths.

## CARE
Houseleeks are extremely drought-resistant, and rarely need watering when grown outdoors. Propagation is very easy, by detaching plantlets from the parent and potting up separately.

**LEAVES**
*The leaves contain a mucilage with similar, but weaker, healing properties to Aloe Vera.*

**LEAVES**
*Thick, fleshy, pointed, spine-tipped leaves, arranged in a rosette. They are predominantly green in colour, with maroon tips, flushing red after prolonged drought.*

**STEM**
*A fleshy runner is produced by the parent plant, at the end of which a plantlet develops.*

## *Symphytum officinale*
# COMFREY
BORAGINACEAE

This remarkable healing herb was once known as knitbone, because the leaves and roots were traditionally used in poultices to mend fractures.

**HABIT** Stout, hardy perennial with bristly, oval, tapering leaves. Purple to white, funnel-shaped flowers in a branched, coiled cluster in summer.

**HEIGHT** 60 cm–1.2 m (2–4 ft).

**SPREAD** 30–60 cm (1–2 ft).

**REMARKS** A vigorous plant, suitable for moist soil in a large herb garden, or a wildflower border. Plant with other large perennials, such as tansy (*Tanacetum vulgare*), soapwort (*Saponaria officinalis*), or sweet cicely (*Myrrhis odorata*).

**STEM**
*Upright and much-branched, with bristly hairs.*

## VARIATIONS

**S. asperum (PRICKLY COMFREY)**
A stout, bristly plant with oval, pointed leaves. Height 1.2–2 m (4–6 ft). Spread 1–1.2 m ( 3–4 ft).

**S. x uplandicum 'VARIEGATUM' (VARIEGATED RUSSIAN COMFREY)**
This hybrid is best grown in semi-shade to avoid scorching of variegated areas. Height 1 m (3 ft). Spread 60 cm (2 ft).

**FLOWERS**
*Drooping, bell-shaped flowers open in succession from coiled clusters of buds.*

## CARE
Consider the planting position carefully, since comfrey is deep-rooted and difficult to move when established, and any pieces of root left behind will regenerate. Cut down dead stems in winter. Comfrey is a rich feeder, so mulch with ample well-rotted manure or compost in the spring.

**FLOWERS**
*Flowers are typically purple to mauve, but plants with white flowers are found occasionally.*

**LEAVES**
*Oval, tapering to the tip, and reaching 25 cm (10 in) long. Lower leaves have long stalks, and become stalkless higher up the stem. They have a stout midrib and a rough, bristly haired surface.*

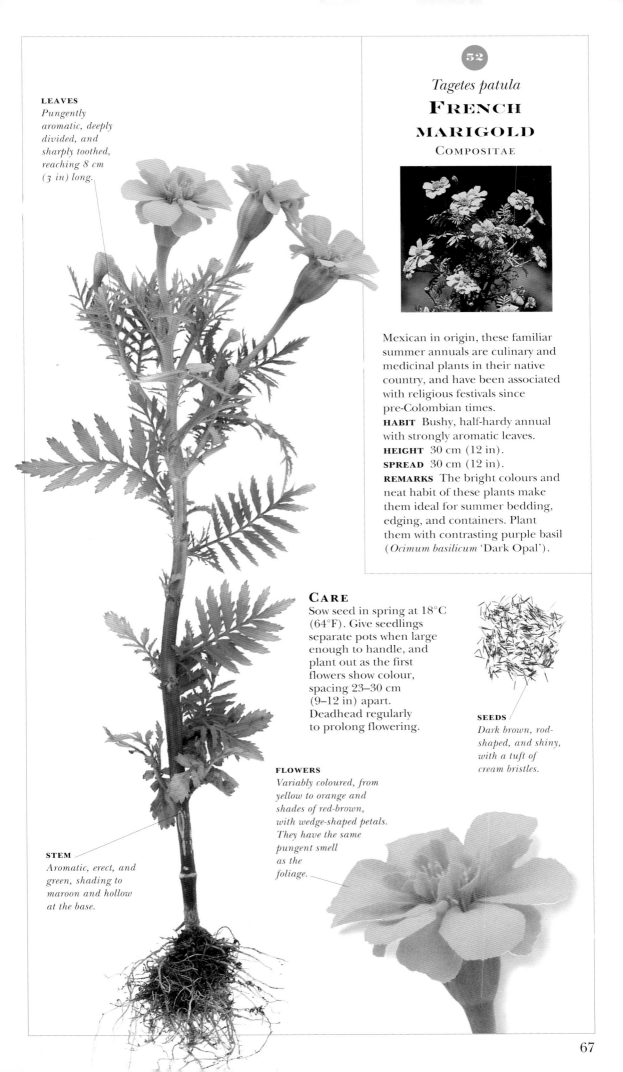

**LEAVES**
*Pungently aromatic, deeply divided, and sharply toothed, reaching 8 cm (3 in) long.*

*Tagetes patula*

# FRENCH MARIGOLD
## COMPOSITAE

Mexican in origin, these familiar summer annuals are culinary and medicinal plants in their native country, and have been associated with religious festivals since pre-Colombian times.

**HABIT** Bushy, half-hardy annual with strongly aromatic leaves.

**HEIGHT** 30 cm (12 in).

**SPREAD** 30 cm (12 in).

**REMARKS** The bright colours and neat habit of these plants make them ideal for summer bedding, edging, and containers. Plant them with contrasting purple basil (*Ocimum basilicum* 'Dark Opal').

## CARE
Sow seed in spring at 18°C (64°F). Give seedlings separate pots when large enough to handle, and plant out as the first flowers show colour, spacing 23–30 cm (9–12 in) apart. Deadhead regularly to prolong flowering.

**SEEDS**
*Dark brown, rod-shaped, and shiny, with a tuft of cream bristles.*

**FLOWERS**
*Variably coloured, from yellow to orange and shades of red-brown, with wedge-shaped petals. They have the same pungent smell as the foliage.*

**STEM**
*Aromatic, erect, and green, shading to maroon and hollow at the base.*

**53**

*Tanacetum vulgare*

# TANSY

COMPOSITAE

Symbolic of bitter Passover herbs, tansy was once used at Easter in custard cakes ("tansies") traditionally consumed by the victor of a handball game played between clergy and congregation.

**HABIT** Hardy perennial with a creeping rootstock and deeply divided, toothed leaves.

**HEIGHT** 60 cm–1.2 m (2–4 ft).

**SPREAD** Indefinite.

**REMARKS** Tansy looks best at the backs of large borders. Plant beside evening primroses (*Oenothera biennis*) and soapwort (*Saponaria officinalis*) for a colourful display in late summer and autumn. The long-lasting flowers are good for cutting.

## VARIATIONS

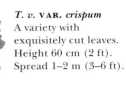

***T. v.* VAR. *crispum***
A variety with exquisitely cut leaves.
Height 60 cm (2 ft).
Spread 1–2 m (3–6 ft).

***T. parthenium***
**(FEVERFEW)**
A strong-smelling, hardy perennial with daisy-like flowers.
Height 60 cm (2 ft).
Spread 45 cm (18 in).

***T. parthenium*
'PLENUM'**
This variety has doublewhite flowers.
It is good for cutting.
Height 60 cm (2 ft).
Spread 45 cm (18 in).

***T. parthenium*
'AUREUM'
(GOLDEN FEVERFEW)**
A handsome plant with bright golden foliage and white daisies.
Height and spread 20–45 cm (8–18 in).

## CARE

Cut down dead stems in winter. Stake in early summer to prevent flopping. Remove excess runners as they appear, and divide the entire clump every second year to control spread. Remove dead flower heads to prevent self-seeding.

**LEAVES**
*Strongly aromatic, dark green leaves, up to 12 cm (5 in) long, divided into deeply toothed leaflets.*

**FLOWERS**
*Aromatic, mustard yellow, button-like flower heads appear in branched, flat-topped clusters.*

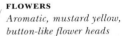

## CARE

Plant 15–23 cm (6–9 in) apart to form a continuous edging. Cut back in spring to maintain a compact habit. Remove dead flower spikes to encourage bushy new growth.

*Teucrium chamaedrys*

# WALL GERMANDER

## LABIATAE

This Mediterranean herb has been used medicinally since ancient times, and was once famed as a cure for gout. It is now considered toxic, but remains very popular as a garden plant.

**HABIT** Hardy, shrubby perennial with a creeping rootstock.

**HEIGHT** 10–25 cm (4–10 in).

**SPREAD** 10–25 cm (4–10 in).

**REMARKS** A neat, modestly spreading plant for containers and for the edges of paths and beds. It is often confused in nurseries with the hedge germanders *T. divaricatum* and *T. x lucidrys.*

**STEM**
*Upright to spreading, slender, dark green, and quite brittle.*

**FLOWERS**
*Small, purple-pink, and two-lipped, in whorls of four to eight, appearing in summer and autumn.*

**LEAVES**
*Oval, often shiny, and neatly lobed, reaching 2 cm (0.75 in) long, and aromatic when crushed. They resemble miniature oak leaves, hence the name* chamaedrys, *meaning "ground oak".*

## 55

*Thymus vulgaris*
# COMMON THYME
### LABIATAE

Though one of the smallest culinary herbs, thyme has no rival for fragrance. The tiny flowers produce large amounts of nectar, making thyme important also as a bee plant.
**HABIT** Variable, hardy shrub with pale mauve to white flowers.
**HEIGHT** 20–30 cm (8–12 in).
**SPREAD** 20–30 cm (8–12 in).
**REMARKS** Small and compact, thyme is indispensable for containers, and as an edging to paths and borders. Grow several different thymes together, varying in habit and colour, and include common thyme for height.

## VARIATIONS

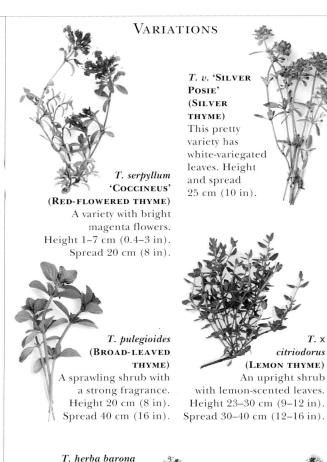

*T. serpyllum* **'COCCINEUS'** (**RED-FLOWERED THYME**)
A variety with bright magenta flowers. Height 1–7 cm (0.4–3 in). Spread 20 cm (8 in).

*T. v.* **'SILVER POSIE'** (**SILVER THYME**)
This pretty variety has white-variegated leaves. Height and spread 25 cm (10 in).

*T. pulegioides* (**BROAD-LEAVED THYME**)
A sprawling shrub with a strong fragrance. Height 20 cm (8 in). Spread 40 cm (16 in).

*T.* x *citriodorus* (**LEMON THYME**)
An upright shrub with lemon-scented leaves. Height 23–30 cm (9–12 in). Spread 30–40 cm (12–16 in).

*T. herba barona* (**CARAWAY THYME**)
A wiry, carpeting thyme with a caraway-nutmeg aroma. Height 1–5 cm (0.4–2 in). Spread 25 cm (10 in).

## CARE
Thyme dislikes hard pruning and wet winters. Trim lightly after flowering to remove dead flower heads and encourage compact growth. Protect thymes from mud-splashing and damp in winter by a layer of grit. Keep plants free of fallen leaves in autumn.

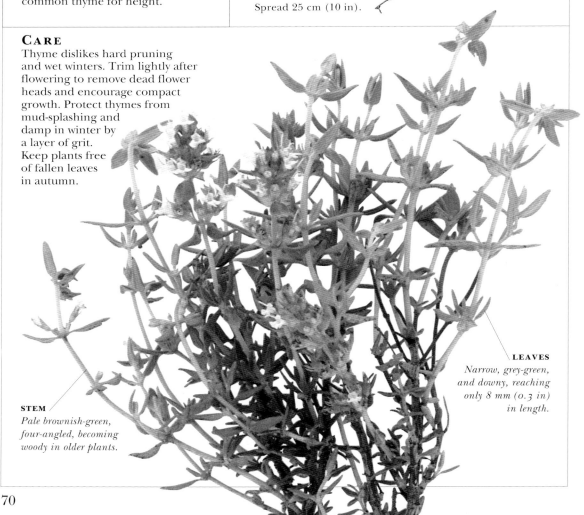

**LEAVES**
*Narrow, grey-green, and downy, reaching only 8 mm (0.3 in) in length.*

**STEM**
*Pale brownish-green, four-angled, becoming woody in older plants.*

## FLOWERS
*Delicate, five-petalled, yellow flowers, up to 3 cm (1.2 in) across, produced in stout spikes in the second summer.*

## CARE
Remove all but one or two dead flower spikes to prevent excessive self-sowing. Weed out seedlings, leaving only the best-placed. Watch out for caterpillars of mullein moths, which seriously damage foliage.

## FLOWER BUDS
*Flowers open in succession from woolly buds from midsummer to mid-autumn.*

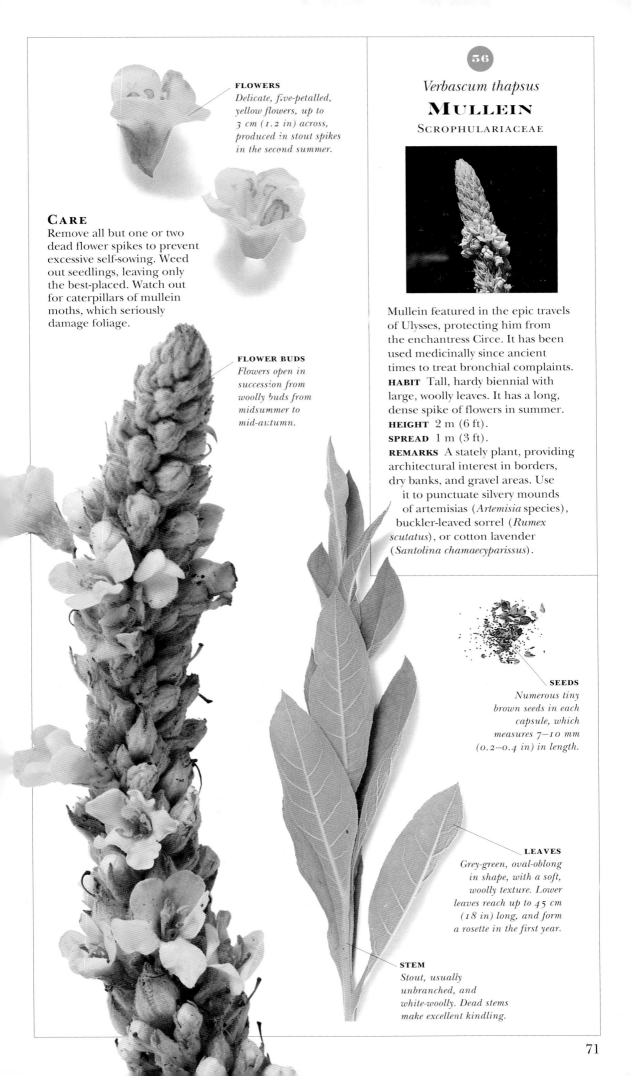

**56**

## *Verbascum thapsus*
# MULLEIN
### SCROPHULARIACEAE

Mullein featured in the epic travels of Ulysses, protecting him from the enchantress Circe. It has been used medicinally since ancient times to treat bronchial complaints.
**HABIT** Tall, hardy biennial with large, woolly leaves. It has a long, dense spike of flowers in summer.
**HEIGHT** 2 m (6 ft).
**SPREAD** 1 m (3 ft).
**REMARKS** A stately plant, providing architectural interest in borders, dry banks, and gravel areas. Use it to punctuate silvery mounds of artemisias (*Artemisia* species), buckler-leaved sorrel (*Rumex scutatus*), or cotton lavender (*Santolina chamaecyparissus*).

## SEEDS
*Numerous tiny brown seeds in each capsule, which measures 7–10 mm (0.2–0.4 in) in length.*

## LEAVES
*Grey-green, oval-oblong in shape, with a soft, woolly texture. Lower leaves reach up to 45 cm (18 in) long, and form a rosette in the first year.*

## STEM
*Stout, usually unbranched, and white-woolly. Dead stems make excellent kindling.*

## *Viburnum opulus*
# GUELDER ROSE
### CAPRIFOLIACEAE

Guelder rose comes from the Dutch province of Gelderland, which was once a centre for wild and cultivated varieties of this shrub. It is also known as crampbark.
**HABIT**  Hardy, deciduous shrub with flat-topped clusters of white flowers in summer, followed by poisonous, scarlet berries.
**HEIGHT**  4 m (12 ft).
**SPREAD**  4 m (12 ft).
**REMARKS**  An excellent garden shrub with delightful flowers and early-ripening, brightly coloured berries. Grow in rich, moist soil with other hedgerow herbs, such as elder (*Sambucus nigra*) and sweet cicely (*Myrrhis odorata*).

**LEAVES**
*Dark green, up to 8 cm (3 in) in length, with three to five lobes, and irregularly toothed.*

## CARE
Plant out of reach of children. Remove any dead wood in spring, and thin out older shoots after flowering. Mulch with well-rotted manure or compost in spring.

**FRUITS**
*Oval to round, and glossy, ripening early to scarlet, in long-stalked clusters.*

**STEM**
*Branches are more or less erect, with smooth twigs and grey bark.*

## VARIATIONS

*Vinca major*

# GREATER PERIWINKLE

APOCYNACEAE

**V. major
'VARIEGATA'**
The most widely
grown variety,
with blue flowers.
Height 45 cm
(18 in). Spread
indefinite.

**V. minor
'ATROPURPUREA'**
An unusual form
with wine-red
flowers. Height
30 cm (12 in).
Spread
indefinite.

**V. minor (LESSER
PERIWINKLE)**
This has narrow
leaves and small
flowers. Height
30 cm (12 in).
Spread
indefinite.

Once known as "sorcerer's violet",
periwinkle was thought to protect
against spirits and spells.
Its poisonous leaves contain
alkaloids, now used in drugs to
treat hardening of the arteries.
**HABIT** Hardy, evergreen subshrub
with glossy leaves and blue flowers.
**HEIGHT** 45 cm (18 in).
**SPREAD** Indefinite.
**REMARKS** One of the best
plants for ground cover in shade,
although it flowers more freely in
a sunny position. Plant beneath
trees and shrubs, or on exposed
banks to bind the soil.

**LEAVES**
*Broadly oval, pointed,
and glossy, reaching
8 cm (3 in) in length,
on short stalks.*

**FLOWERS**
*Blue, propeller-
shaped, and about
4 cm (1.6 in) across,
appearing on short,
erect flowering stems.*

**STEM**
*Long, green, and slender,
with an arching or trailing
habit, rooting at the tips.*

**CARE**
To control spread, remove
colonizing stems as they
appear, and cut back hard
in autumn or winter.

## *Viola odorata*
# SWEET VIOLET
### VIOLACEAE

Violets were at their height of popularity during Roman times, and again in the 19th century. Many of the finest varieties, grown for cut flowers, perfumery, and crystallizing, became extinct during World Wars I and II.

**HABIT** Hardy, spreading perennial with dark purple, sweetly scented flowers from late winter to spring.

**HEIGHT** 15 cm (6 in).

**SPREAD** 30 cm (12 in).

**REMARKS** A delightful plant for the edges of paths and borders, or for open ground near shrubs. Grow with other small hedgerow herbs, such as woodruff (*Galium odoratum*) and wild strawberry (*Fragaria vesca*).

## VARIATION

***V. tricolor*** (**HEARTSEASE**)
An easy, delightful viola for borders and containers. Unscented, miniature pansies appear in spring and summer. Height and spread 15–23 cm (6–9 in).

**FLOWERS**
*These have two upper and three lower petals. Typical violet scent is dependent on a volatile oil in the flowers, containing ionone.*

**SEEDS**
*Round, three-lobed capsules split open when ripe, releasing tiny, light brown, oval seeds.*

**LEAVES**
*Broadly oval to heart-shaped, up to 6 cm (2.4 in) in length, with long stalks and indented margins.*

## CARE
Mulch with well-rotted manure, compost, or leaf mould in winter. Sweet violets are easily propagated by removing individual plantlets that form on runners. Deadhead to prolong flowering.

**STEM**
*Tough, brown rhizomes and long, creeping runners.*

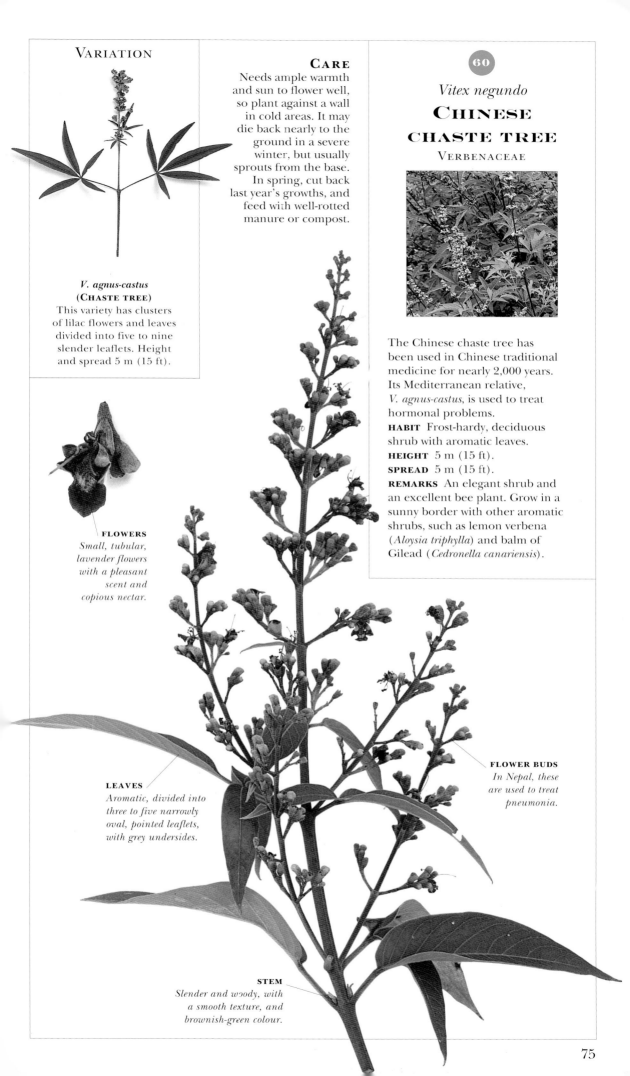

## CARE
Needs ample warmth
and sun to flower well,
so plant against a wall
in cold areas. It may
die back nearly to the
ground in a severe
winter, but usually
sprouts from the base.
In spring, cut back
last year's growths, and
feed with well-rotted
manure or compost.

**60**

*Vitex negundo*

# CHINESE CHASTE TREE
### VERBENACEAE

*V. agnus-castus*
(**CHASTE TREE**)
This variety has clusters
of lilac flowers and leaves
divided into five to nine
slender leaflets. Height
and spread 5 m (15 ft).

The Chinese chaste tree has
been used in Chinese traditional
medicine for nearly 2,000 years.
Its Mediterranean relative,
*V. agnus-castus*, is used to treat
hormonal problems.
**HABIT** Frost-hardy, deciduous
shrub with aromatic leaves.
**HEIGHT** 5 m (15 ft).
**SPREAD** 5 m (15 ft).
**REMARKS** An elegant shrub and
an excellent bee plant. Grow in a
sunny border with other aromatic
shrubs, such as lemon verbena
(*Aloysia triphylla*) and balm of
Gilead (*Cedronella canariensis*).

**FLOWERS**
*Small, tubular,
lavender flowers
with a pleasant
scent and
copious nectar.*

**FLOWER BUDS**
*In Nepal, these
are used to treat
pneumonia.*

**LEAVES**
*Aromatic, divided into
three to five narrowly
oval, pointed leaflets,
with grey undersides.*

**STEM**
*Slender and woody, with
a smooth texture, and
brownish-green colour.*

# OTHER VARIATIONS

### 9
*Buxus sempervirens*
**BOX**
BOXACEAE
PAGE 21

**B. s. 'Latifolia Maculata'**
A handsome box for golden colour schemes, with gold-marbled foliage and bright yellow new growth.
Height 2 m (6 ft).
Spread 1–1.5 m (3–5 ft).

### 10
*Calendula officinalis*
**MARIGOLD**
COMPOSITAE
PAGE 22

A number of compact, double-flowered cultivars are sold as seed. They can be grown and used in the same ways as the species, and make excellent cut flowers. One of the most widely available is **C. o. 'Fiesta Gitana'**, with flowers in shades of orange, yellow, cream, and bronze. Height and spread 30 cm (12 in).

### 15
*Echinacea purpurea*
**CONEFLOWER**
COMPOSITAE
PAGE 27

**E. p. 'White Swan'**
A smaller plant than the species, with large, white daisies. It will tolerate drier conditions.
Height 45–60 cm (18–24 in). Spread 30 cm (12 in).

### 16
*Eschscholzia californica*
**CALIFORNIAN POPPY**
PAPAVERACEAE
PAGE 28

A number of compact, colourful cultivars are sold as seed. They can be grown and used in the same ways as the species, and make excellent cut flowers. An example is **E. c. 'Monarch'**, which produces single and semi-double flowers in shades of pink, carmine, orange, and yellow. Height and spread 23 cm (9 in).

### 19
*Fragaria vesca*
**WILD STRAWBERRY**
ROSACEAE
PAGE 31

Two very different cultivars are **F. v. 'Multiplex'**, with double flowers, and **F. v. 'Baron Solemacher'**, a heavy-fruiting plant with a neat, non-running habit. For both of these cultivars: height 25 cm (10 in), spread 20 cm (8 in).

### 1
*Agastache foeniculum*
**ANISE HYSSOP**
LABIATAE
PAGE 12

**A. f. 'Alabaster'**
A handsome, white-flowered cultivar. Height 45–60 cm (18–24 in). Spread 30 cm (12 in).

### 3
*Allium schoenoprasum*
**CHIVES**
LILIACEAE
PAGE 14

**A. tuberosum**
(Garlic or Chinese chives)
A useful late-flowering herb, with flattened, garlic-flavoured leaves, and clusters of starry white flowers from late summer to autumn.
Height and spread 50 cm (20 in).

### 7
*Artemisia* species
**ARTEMISIA**
COMPOSITAE
PAGE 18

**A. lactiflora Guizhou Group**
This cultivar has dark maroon stems, which set off the cream flowers. Height 1.2–1.5 m (4–5 ft). Spread 50 cm (20 in).

**A. 'Powis Castle'**
A dwarf, non-flowering artemisia with silver foliage, and a compact shape. It makes good ground cover or informal hedging for dry, sunny sites. Height 60 cm–1 m (2–3 ft). Spread 1.2 m (4 ft).

### 8
*Borago officinalis*
**BORAGE**
BORAGINACEAE
PAGE 20

**B. o. 'Alba'**
The pure white flowers of this borage are perfect for white gardens, and complement pastels, such as soft pink balm of Gilead (*Cedronella canariensis*) and mauve goat's rue (*Galega officinalis*).
Height 30 cm–1 m (1–3 ft). Spread 15–30 cm (6–12 in).

### 20
*Galega officinalis*
**GOAT'S RUE**
LEGUMINOSAE
PAGE 32

**G. o. 'Alba'**
A popular cultivar with spikes of pure white flowers.
Height 1–1.5 m (3–5 ft).
Spread 60 cm–1 m (2–3 ft).

### 22
*Hedera helix*
**IVY**
ARALIACEAE
PAGE 34

There are over 300 cultivars, grown for ground cover or as climbers for garden use, or as pot plants, especially in mixed plantings for containers. Good examples include:

**H. h. 'Erecta'**
This forms upright bushes of small, triangular leaves. Height 1 m (3 ft). Spread 1.2 m (4 ft).

**H. h. 'Glacier'**
A small ivy with white-edged leaves, marbled silver-grey. Less hardy than the species, but excellent for pot plants and ground cover under glass.

**H. h. 'Goldheart'**
An outstanding climber for walls in good light, with yellow-centred, dark green leaves. Height 6 m (20 ft). Spread 3 m (10 ft).

### 23
*Helianthus annuus*
**SUNFLOWER**
COMPOSITAE
PAGE 35

**H. a. 'Italian White'**
A bushy plant with branched stems of small, black-centred, creamy-white flowers. Height 1.2 m (4 ft). Spread 20 cm (8 in).

**H. a. 'Teddy Bear'**
A dwarf sunflower with fully double flowers. Height 60 cm (2 ft). Spread 30 cm (12 in).

### 29
*Melissa officinalis*
**LEMON BALM**
LABIATAE
PAGE 42

**M. o. 'All Gold'**
This has yellow leaves. It should be planted in good light, with midday shade, to prevent scorching.
Height 30–60 cm (1–2 ft).
Spread 30–45 cm (12–18 in).

*Mentha* species
**MINT**
LABIATAE
PAGE 43

**M. × piperita**
(Peppermint)
A vigorous hybrid with red-tinged
stems, and dark green,
often purple-flushed leaves.
Height 30 cm–1 m (1–3 ft).
Spread indefinite.

**M. requienii**
(Corsican mint)
The tiniest of mints, with creeping,
thread-like stems, and pungently
scented leaves. It often self-sows,
even if the parent plant does not
survive winter. Height 2–10 cm
(0.8–4 in). Spread indefinite.

*Monarda didyma*
**BERGAMOT**
LABIATAE
PAGE 44

**M. d. 'Cambridge Scarlet'**
The most popular bergamot,
with vivid red flowers above bright
green, aromatic leaves. Height 1 m
(3 ft). Spread 45 cm (18 in).

*Myrtus communis*
**MYRTLE**
MYRTACEAE
PAGE 46

**M. c. 'Variegata'**
An attractive plant for containers,
with leaves variegated grey-green
and cream. Height 3–5 m
(10–15 ft). Spread 3 m (10 ft).

*Papaver rhoeas*
**POPPY**
PAPAVERACEAE
PAGE 52

**P. r. 'Mother of Pearl'**
One of many cultivars available as
seed, with pastel-coloured flowers
in unusual shades of grey, blue,
lilac, and pink. Height 25–38 cm
(10–15 in). Spread 20 cm (8 in).

**P. somniferum 'Danebrog'**
This flamboyant opium poppy has
bright red, often fringed petals,
each with a white basal blotch.
Height 75 cm (30 in).
Spread 30 cm (12 in).

*Pelargonium* species
**SCENTED PELARGONIUM**
GERANIACEAE
PAGE 53

Other pelargoniums to grow
include: *P. crispum* (Lemon
pelargonium) and its variegated

form, *P. crispum* 'Variegatum',
with small, crinkled, lemon-scented
leaves; *P.* 'Fragrans' (Nutmeg
pelargonium), which has small,
silky leaves and a spicy scent;
*P.* 'Graveolens', a rose-scented
pelargonium with deeply lobed
leaves, similar to those of the
variegated *P.* 'Lady Plymouth';
and *P. tomentosum* (Peppermint
pelargonium), a spreading plant,
tolerant of partial shade, with large,
velvety leaves, and a strong
peppermint aroma. As container
plants, all can be kept to 30–60 cm
(1–2 ft) in height and spread by
regular pinching out and pruning.

*Salvia officinalis*
**SAGE**
LABIATAE
PAGE 60

**S. o. 'Albiflora'**
The white-flowered form of
common sage is an elegant plant
for silver, white, and pastel colour
schemes. Height 60–80 cm
(24–32 in). Spread 1 m (3 ft).

**S. o. 'Tricolor'**
A sage with grey-green leaves,
irregularly variegated pink and
ivory. Being smaller and less
vigorous than the species, it is better
for mixed plantings in containers.
Height and spread 45–60 cm
(18–24 in).

*Sambucus nigra*
**ELDER**
CAPRIFOLIACEAE
PAGE 61

**S. n. 'Aurea'**
(Golden elder)
A resilient golden-leaved shrub
that withstands hard frost and full
sun. Young foliage is bright yellow,
ageing lime-green. Height and
spread 6 m (20 ft).

**S. n. 'Marginata'**
The leaves of this elder have
irregular creamy-white margins.
Height and spread 6 m (20 ft).

*Tagetes patula*
**FRENCH MARIGOLD**
COMPOSITAE
PAGE 67

Many variants are available as seed
or as young plants for summer
bedding. They include:

**T. p. 'Honeycomb'**, with double,
deep orange flowers, edged yellow.
Height and spread 25 cm (10 in).

**T. p. 'Naughty Marietta'**, which
has single yellow flowers with
a maroon blotch on each petal.
Height and spread 25 cm (10 in).

*Teucrium chamaedrys*
**WALL GERMANDER**
LABIATAE
PAGE 69

**T. × lucidrys**
(Hedge germander)
This hybrid germander has a more
upright habit and glossier, more
leathery leaves than *T. chamaedrys*.
It makes a good dwarf hedge and
there is also a variegated form.
Height 30 cm (12 in).
Spread 25 cm (10 in).

*Thymus* species
**THYME**
LABIATAE
PAGE 70

**T. 'Doone Valley'**
A bushy creeper with irregular
yellow variegation, red-tinged in
winter, and a lemon scent. It tends
to revert, so cut plain green stems
for flavouring. Height 8 cm (3 in).
Spread 20 cm (8 in).

**T. pseudolanuginosus**
(Woolly thyme)
A distinctive creeping thyme with
grey-green, woolly leaves and pale
pink flowers. Height 1–2.5 cm
(0.4–1 in). Spread 45 cm (18 in).

*Viburnum opulus*
**GUELDER ROSE**
CAPRIFOLIACEAE
PAGE 72

**V. o. 'Aureum'**
A compact variant with golden
leaves. Plant in semi-shade since
the foliage tends to scorch in
full sun. Height and spread 4 m
(12 ft).

**V. o. 'Roseum'**
(Snowball bush)
A favourite garden shrub with ball-
shaped flower heads, composed
entirely of sterile flowers, and
bearing no berries. Height and
spread 4 m (12 ft).

*Vinca major*
**GREATER PERIWINKLE**
APOCYNACEAE
PAGE 73

**V. minor 'Azurea Flore Pleno'**
A very pretty variant with double
blue flowers. Height 30 cm
(12 in). Spread indefinite.

# INDEX

# ACKNOWLEDGMENTS

**PHOTOGRAPHY CREDITS**
Key: t = top; tl = top left; tr = top right; tc = top centre; cl = centre left; cr = centre right;
b = bottom; bl = bottom left; br = bottom right.

Photographs by Peter Anderson, Eric Crichton, Philip Dowell, Neil Fletcher, Steve Gorton,
Derek Hall, Stephen Hayward, Dave King, Andrew McKnobb, David Murray, and
Matthew Ward, except:

Deni Bown: 9br; 10cl; 11cr; 12tl; 14tl; 16tl; 17tr; 21tr and tl; 22tl; 23tr; 26tl; 27tr; 30tl; 31tr;
32tl; 34tl; 36tl; 38tl; 46cl and tl; 47tr; 48tl; 53tr and tc; 54tl; 55tr; 56tr; 58tl and tc; 59cr; 60tl;
61tl and tr; 63tl and tr; 65tl; 66tl; 69tr; 70tl and cr; 71tr; 72tl; 73tr and tl; 74tl; 75tr.
Bridgeman Art Library/British Library, London: 6b.
Geoff Dann: 24tl; 51tr.
E.T. Archive/Bodleian Library: 6t.
Royal Botanic Garden, Edinburgh: 20tl.
Neil Campbell Sharp: 8cl.
Clive Nichols: 2.
Harry Smith Collection: 10c; 39tr; 52tl.


**Design assistance:** Wendy Bartlet and Sarah Goodwin.

**Editorial assistance:** Annabel Morgan

**Picture research:** Lorna Ainger.

**DK Picture Library:** Ola Rudowska.